A History of
The Parish of
MORLEY
Derbyshire

The Morley Village History Committee

MOORLEY'S BIBLE & Bookshop Ltd.

Copyright 1977
Morley Village History Committee

ISBN 0 86071 033 5

Published on behalf of
Morley Village History Committee
MOORLEY'S BIBLE & BOOKSHOP LTD., ILKESTON.

I N D E X

	Page No.
Preface	5
The Parish of Morley	7
The Village Itself	13
The Parish Records	27
The Churchwardens' Accounts	28
Items from the Parish Registers	104
The Parish Constable	45
Roads	49
Poor Relief in Morley	37
Morley's Schools	63
Morley Moor Chapel	68
The Reverend Robert Wilmot	55
The Reverend Samuel Fox	89
Within Living Memory	69
The Village Today	92
The Geographical Background	97
Appendices	103 & 106
Conclusion	108
Acknowledgments	107

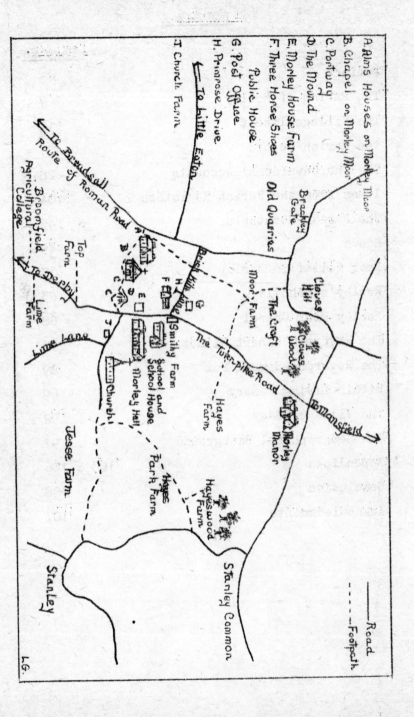

PREFACE

We began this history of Morley in 1963 after two of Morley's Women's Institute members had attended a meeting on 'Derbyshire Place Names' by Dr. Kenneth Cameron, and arranged for the Derbyshire Federation of Women's Institutes by Miss N. Middleton, W.E.A. Organiser for Derby.

We attended a series of meetings during 1963 in Morley, our tutor being Miss R. Tulloch, B.A., who told us how and where to look for information and also helped in collecting and putting the notes into some order. We are very grateful to her for all her advice and enthusiasm, and to Miss N. Middleton who arranged the meetings for her help and encouragement.

To write a complete history of a parish is a great undertaking. We were very much a group of amateurs and we hope that this is only a beginning and that others may venture and continue the search. We made an attempt to search the old parish registers, books and newspapers as best we could, but because of the costs involved it was not possible to get it printed.

The Women's Institute members who helped in one way or another to compile these notes were:- Miss D. Topham, Mrs. M. Slack, Mrs. L. Peach, Mrs. I. Hammersley, Mrs. L. Giblin, Mrs. K. Drinkwater and Mrs. E. Bestwick, and we were assisted by Mr. F. Bestwick, Mr. M. Bladon, Mr. and Mrs. J. Dawes and Mr. R. Hammersley.

We should like to record our thanks to Mr. R. Dilks for his notes and map on the geology of the area in the original manuscript; and Mr. F. S. Ogden, F.R.I.C.S. (Churchwarden) of Morley Church for his drawings and notes on the Rectory and the Almshouses, also in the original manuscript, and to the Villagers themselves for their patience in answering innumerable questions.

We should also like to thank the then Rector of Morley, Canon R.P. Stacy Waddy for allowing us access to the old parish registers (which were our main source of information), and for his help and interest, also the staffs of the Derby Borough and County Libraries.

As this is the Silver Jubilee year of our Queen's accession, we thought this would be an appropriate time to publish this as a tribute to this historic occasion, and a fitting reminder of the part Morley and its people have played in the past. We are indebted to those in the parish and their friends outside and to the present Women's Institute members who have encouraged us to prepare this for print.

Eva E. Bestwick

1977

THE PARISH OF MORLEY

Morley is a very scattered village. Near the church there is a nucleus of houses but there are other settlements separated from this by over a mile. It seems probable that this pattern of settlement is a very old one and grew up because of the ring of springs that surround the slightly higher ground of the church and the moor. This is substantiated by the fact that the roads are through roads linking one town with another, rather than linking the various settlements of Morley together. Access from one part of the village to another is still in many cases along footpaths and bridle-paths; the houses therefore were positioned before the roads, and developed their own connecting links.

Morley is certainly a very old parish. The possession of the land can be traced from deeds, copies of which can be seen in the Derby Borough Library. Before 1066, in the days of Ethelred the Unready, the land of Morley was presented to Burton Abbey. Through the centuries it passed first to Henry de Ferrers and then to the Abbot of Chester from whom it was held by the Morleys, and the Stathums, until finally it came into the possession of the Sacheverells. In 1786 at the time of the Enclosure Award the joint lords of the manor were Sir Hugh Bateman, Sitwell and Sacheverell Pole. Memorials to all these families can be seen in the church.

The Use of the Land

Morley has always been a farming village. In the north of the parish there are the stone quarries and just over the boundary in Smalley there has been a certain amount of coal mining. In Morley too coal has been found, and Sir Charles Petrie quotes from "English Industries of the Middle Ages":[1] 'One of the earliest references to coal damp is in connection with the death in 1322 of a woman, one Emma, daughter of William Culhare, who was killed by 'le Damp' while drawing water from a 'colepyt' at Morley, Derbyshire. The Reverend Charles Kerry in his "History of Smalley" also refers to a pit in Morley in 1723, but the adventure was obviously a failure and must have been soon abandoned. Glover's "History of Derbyshire"[2] states: 'the colliery was situated one third of a mile East of the town'. In the past there has been some opencast mining in the village.

Land however, has been the main source of income. Probably most of the land was pasture, for as late as 1843 the Tithe Award shows Morley as having 1820 acres of land of which only 500 acres were arable. In the Middle Ages the usual pattern was that the arable land was split into three large fields in each of which Villagers would have strips. The method of ploughing these strips in order to keep them separate has left a distinctive pattern of ridge and furrow which can be seen very clearly in some parts of England. In Morley the field behind the Almshouses shows traces of this. As well as the three fields, the villages had meadows for hay and a stretch of common land. The common land was used for grazing by all the beasts, and people who had no strips but who owned a few sheep or hens or a cow, could graze their animals on the common with those belonging to the richer men of the village. Gradually land was enclosed i.e. fenced-in into the individually owned farms that we know today. Probably the arable land in Morley was enclosed by private agreements in the sixteenth and seventeenth centuries, because the Enclosure Award of 1786 which was an Act of Parliament, seems to refer to Morley Moor which must have been the old common land of Morley. Unfortunately the map which would have made clear the exact boundaries of the enclosure is missing. The field name "close" refers to the earliest enclosures, or to land reclaimed from forest or moor. In the field names in the Enclosure Award are names such as Barley's Close, Broom Close, Brick Kiln Close, Burrows Close and Hovel Close.

The Parliamentary enclosures did lead to hardship because only those who could produce proof of their rights were entitled to a share of the newly enclosed land, and the result was that many poor people who had managed to keep going while they had the opportunity to graze their animals on the common, were now compelled to become labourers. This change was generally approved. Glover in his "History and Gazeteer of Derbyshire"[3] writes in the nineteenth century: 'the less business of his own that a labourer has which should at any time cause him to leave his regular employ and be his own master the better for his habits, his family and his country'. The Reverend Robert Wilmot[4] who was the Rector of the parish during the time of the enclosures also felt that the free use of the common encouraged bad habits. ...'Upon the inclosure the cottagers' families who were scantily supported by keeping a few geese and sheep on the commons and thereby enabled to live in idleness were compelled to go out to service'.

Robert Wilmot had written these remarks at the time of the census of 1801 and from the census we discover there were seven smallholders and their families and fifteen farmworkers in Morley. Wages at this time were about 1s.6d. a day or 9s.0d. for a full week, but in the winter labourers were put on lower wages since not so much work could be done. Occasionally in a bad winter a kind-hearted employer like the Reverend Mr. Wilmot would not reduce the wages, but even at the summer level a family could only exist if the women and children worked. We have no direct evidence of how any Morley family spent its money, but for interest we give a week's 'shopping list' from the 'English Countrywoman':-

Bread	9s. 0d
Potatoes	1s. 0d
Tea	2d
Sugar	3½d
Salt	½d
Butter	4½d
Cheese	3d
Soap	2d
Blue	½d
Coal and Wood	9d
Candles	3d
Rent	1s. 2d
	13s. 6d

Others in the village were better off of course. There was Thomas Chambers, a stockinger, who 'earned by his own confession not less than thirty-five shillings a week' (Robert Wilmot, Parish Registers 1795). Among the farmers the late eighteenth and nineteenth centuries were a time of great prosperity as can be seen if one looks at the rebuilding and extension of farmhouses that took place at that time.. Morley House Farm, Morley Moor Farm, Hayes Park Farm and Jesse Farm all bear witness to this. So too do the Tithe Books; in the late eighteenth century the tithe was about £140 a year, by 1843 this sum had more than doubled. In the Tithe book of 1843 eighteen landowners are listed including the Trustees of the Turnpike Trust but nearly all the land belonged to the executors of Sir Hugh Bateman.

The two chief sources of information about the land of Morley are the Enclosure Award of 1786 (which has no map) and the Tithe Award of 1843 which has a map showing and naming every field in the parish. "Derbyshire Place Names"[5] by Dr. Kenneth Cameron lists some of the names that occur, for instance Park Farm, Morleymore and Morley Hall are all named before 1600 and

Lime Farm and Morley Lime are probably very ancient names. Lime 'lemo' is an old British (i.e. pre-Roman) word for elm and these names it is suggested preserve the idea of the extensive forest region which once covered south-east Derbyshire.

The register of births, marriages and deaths also mentions 'Closes', 'Clooves' and 'Cloves' Hill as early as 1607 and 'Morley Hayes' in 1612.

It is interesting also to find family names that have survived and are known to us today as place names:-

    1660 Elizabeth '<u>Brumfield</u>'
    1678 Widow '<u>Brackley</u>' of Horsley Park Gate
    1622 George '<u>Ferrebie</u>'

It is from these records that a tiny story emerges of a man who lived in Morley and except for these church records is completely unknown. But from these three entries and the readers' imagination a whole section of his life can be pictured:-

    1622 Oct. Margery, wife of George Ferrebie buried.
    1624 Apr. George Ferrebie and Tarcye Chester both of Morley married.
    1630 Mar. George Ferrebie, a poore old labouring man was buried.

And as with George Ferrebie, every entry in these registers has this interest, that it is about people who lived here in this parish, and whose lives are barely known apart from these brief notes.

In 1774 John Ward, the curate, made a census of the village apparently for his own interest, but a later entry says that this was incomplete. In 1801 the government ordered a census to be made for all England and an accurate return was made of all houses and families.

Ward lists only twenty-six families although we know that there were forty-nine houses, but he splits the parish into the Town (the houses at the top of Church Lane), the bottom of the Town (bottom of Church Lane), the Moor, the Lime and The Park. The Enclosure Act meant that some houses on the common were pulled down, but the Reverend Robert Wilmot notes that more houses were built by 1801. Occupations are mentioned on the census returns and of course most people earned their living from the land, but there seems to have been a number doing other work and perhaps some of the farmworkers eked out the bad weather with a different job.

In the 1774 census apart from the farmworkers, there was a butcher, a nailer, two shoe makers, a grocer and a framework knitter, and to this the 1801 census adds a weaver, a huckster, a victualler, a blacksmith, two more framework knitters and a ropemaker. The baptismal register (which adopted a new form of entry in the nineteenth century showing the occupation of the father) shows a wheelwright and gamekeeper in 1815, and in 1838 there was a toll collector.

Considering the importance of the quarries there is very little reference throughout the church records to masons. No-one in 1774 or 1801 worked in the quarries, and even in the later records the only mention of a mason is of one who lived on Breadsall Moor, so perhaps the workers tended to live outside the parish. Glover's "Gazeteer of Derbyshire in 1831" gives an account of the stone quarries and records that the grindstones, from 18" to 4' in diameter were exported by canal presumably from Little Eaton so it is possible that the workers came from that area.

By 1851 there were fifty-seven houses and 286 inhabitants (144 male and 142 female) and in 1857 Morley had two shop-keepers, a wheelwright, a victualler and blacksmith, and a framework knitter. Ten years later in 1861 two more houses had been built, but the inhabitants had decreased to 230 and included a butcher and victualler living at the Three Horse Shoes.

THE THREE HORSE SHOES.

CHAPTER 2

THE VILLAGE ITSELF

Some of Morley's history can still be seen in its old buildings and in the pattern of the old roads. Morley is still a village, drawing its livelihood mainly from farming, and unlike a town where new factories and housing estates obliterate the old history, in Morley one can still feel a sense of continuity with the past.

We give here a list of some of the places of interest to be seen.

The Portway

In pre-Roman England there were a number of trackways criss-crossing the country and one of these, the Portway, leads past Morley Church and can still be traced in the footpath across to the Almshouses. To Mr. P.H. Currey[6] must go the credit for recognising the antiquity of the Morley section of the road. In 1912 he published some notes in which he describes the road[7], as it is approached from the Coxbench side. 'After crossing the brook it again mounts to Morley Moor, in part as a footpath, but after crossing the Roman Rykneld Street, it again becomes a bridle road, and as such goes through a fairly direct course through Morley and Stanley to Dale Abbey. On Morley Moor the road takes a sharp bend round the well-known moated mound. Whether the bend in the road fixed the site of the Mound or whether the Mound fixed the site of the road it is hard to say, but there is an obvious connection between the two which is proof of great antiquity.'

Rykneld Street

The system of Roman roads in England has been well mapped and the section that passes through Morley leads from Little Chester through

Breadsall passing northwards. The present road from Breadsall, narrow, straight, paying no regards to the contours and quite different in character from the carefully graded turnpike road on the other side of the Moor, represents the course of Rykneld Street. Just past Almshouses Lane the present road leaves the old road which can still be traced crossing the fields to the east towards Morley Moor Farm. Part of it was excavated and the following account is taken from the Derby Archaeological and Natural History Society Journal volume 8 by W.T. Watkin:[8]

'A section was examined to the south of Morley Moor and the road was found to have a foundation of large irregular sandstone blocks 6 inches thick and 1 - 2 feet square, laid for a width of 18 feet 10 inches. Upon this was a layer of small pieces of sandstone 4 - 6 inches across with a surfacing of small stones and gravel 3 - 4 inches thick.' Presumably the sandstone came from the local quarries and altogether the road must have been a substantial and impressive sight.

The Mound

One of the most unusual and interesting things to see in Morley is the strange moated mound which lies on the path leading from the Almshouses to the Church - the route of the Portway. It is now covered with trees but still almost surrounded by a moat. It stands about twenty feet high and the platform on top is about five feet across. What the actual origin was no-one can say for sure. W. Andrew in the "Victory County History"[9] considers it to be 'a perfect specimen of a defensive mound'. But J.W. Allen in an article in The Derbyshire Countryside[10] argues that it could never have been big enough for use by more than a dozen men, and dates it much later as a look-out post. 'It is at the highest point of the Moor and from the

- 14 -

top a very extensive landscape is seen. The approach of a company along the highway could readily be seen or detected by the movement of birds. When the district was part of the Duffield Frith and scene of royal hunting parties, the Mound could well have served for locating the whereabouts of a party.

Mr. Cockerton[11] of Bakewell has a different theory. He suggests that it was raised by the Romans to help in their survey for Rykneld Street which of course lies quite near. He writes, 'I am inclined to think that this Mound was raised up on the old route (the Portway) as a deliberate obstruction by people who did not care whether the old road fell into disuse or not, and who were obsessed with providing a new road system'. Mr. Cockerton adds, 'I sometimes wonder whether the ancient Mound is really the site of the Morelestone mentioned in 1086, i.e. the stone at Morley. Dr. K. Cameron in "Place Names of Derbyshire" says that the stone is unknown, but the meeting place was still there in 1300.

Whatever theory one supports it is difficult to see how conclusive proof can be forthcoming. In the meantime the Mound stands silent - one of the question marks of local history.

The Church

Obviously this is one of the buildings in a village to which a historian first turns. There have, however, been admirable histories of the church already written by the Reverend Samuel Fox[12] and by Mrs. Compton Bracebridge,[13] and so what follows is only a suggestion of what can be found.

There is, according to Mr. Cockerton evidence of a Saxon building where the present church now stands by the old lane leading off the Mansfield Road. Proof of the historic foundation of the church was discovered when work was proceeding on the wall of the nave, when there was uncovered the original arcades dating from the time of either Stephen or that of Henry II.

Among the many treasures of the present church are the famous brasses on the tombs of the Sacheverell family; the seventeenth-century Communion Plate given by a member of that family and the medieval glass in the North windows of the Sacheverell chapel which were brought by Francis Pole of Radbourne when Dale Abbey monastery was dissolved in the reign of Henry VIII. The church also contains the tomb of Katherine Babington, grandmother of Anthony, whose conspiracy to rescue Mary Queen of Scots from captivity brought him to the scaffold. Two tombs in the church bring vividly to light the tragedy in human terms of the religious differences of the seventeenth century. Two Sacheverell brothers died within a few years of each other in the late seventeenth century, Jacinth 'in the true orthodox faith' i.e. the Roman Catholic, and Jonathas 'a staunch supporter of the Puritan ideals'. The elder brother Jacinth, who founded the Almshouses bequeathed the property to a relative of the Barton line to the exclusion of his brother.

The Rectory

There is a note in the church registers that in 1740 'the Parsonage House was burnt down so the present house is that noted in the 1774 census and by Bagshaw in his "History and Gazeteer"[14] of 1846 as 'a neat modern mansion undergoing considerable alterations'.

We are indebted to Mr.F.S. Ogden[15] for giving

THE ALMS HOUSES.

further information about the Rectory. 'The octagonal bay in the dining room, the cloaks and the part of the kitchen on the north side are additions to the original house together with the relative parts of the floors above, and may be part of the 'considerable alterations' noted by Bagshaw.'

He comments on the working portion of the house where provision was made for making cheeses, pickling meat, curing bacon and brewing beer. There was a large brick oven and a brewing copper. An original stone cheese press has been left in position in the larder. There still remains a portion of a small complete range of farm buildings at the back of the Rectory on the glebe farm land and approached only by the main drive, so presumably the glebe land was farmed by the Rector himself. One of the rectors, the Reverend Robert Wilmot (late eighteenth century) was certainly well acquainted with farm prices.

Mr. Ogden mentions other details which throw light on the life lived in that eighteenth century house - the deep well beneath the kitchen floor (now filled in), the brick oven and the brewing copper which were in the next adjoining outbuildings, the brick oven extending out into the walled backyard in the form of a small brick building having a pitched tile roof. A flight of stairs led from the back kitchen to a chamber over the larders known as 'the apple chamber'. Access had been made to the top of these stairs from a lobby in the bedroom. There were also arched beer and wine cellars. Some of the floors of the upper room are 'plaster floors' i.e. a form of concrete laid on reeds.

In 1959 the Rectory became the Diocesan Retreat and Conference House when considerable internal alterations were made to the building. The ground floor has a large library which can be used for lectures and discussions, a common room which was the old drawing room, a newly created kitchen block and dining room, and a small chapel austere and simple in character.

The roof of the Rectory was stripped of its original tiles and all the sound ones were reused. These old tiles had no holes for nailing, and as it was considered necessary to have some rows of tiles nailed to the new laths for security, each fifth row of tiles was replaced with new holed tiles. It was expected that these would darken to a tone comparable with the old tiles in time.

The Village Cross

The shaft of an old churchyard cross stands near to the vestry door and was considerably shortened to receive a sundial which was placed upon it in 1762. In the Rectory grounds there is the shaft of another cross - the Butter or barter Cross enclosed from a public green in the eighteenth century. This name suggests that Morley was something of a local market centre but there is no documentary evidence to back this up. The cross was restored in 1916 by Mr. H. Topham of Morley Hall when the figures of Our Lady and Child were placed on the shaft.

Tithe Barn and Dovecote

Behind the church stands an old barn and dovecote dating from the seventeenth century and possibly originally part of the outbuildings of the Old Morley Hall, home of the Sacheverells when they lived in Morley.

The ground floor has since been used as coach house and stabling by the various Rectors, and at one time the grooms are believed to have lived in the upper storey. It has also been used for storing grain.

Towards the end of the last century the upper storey was adapted so that it could be used by the village for social activities. The present wooden floor was placed over the old plaster one and the dovecote served as the kitchen. An additional covered staircase was built at the east end of the building presumably to conform with safety regulations. This room became known as the Recreation Room and still is the only parish room for social events. The roof was re-tiled and the beams strengthened in 1963 and alterations were made to the dovecote during 1965. This was thought necessary as part of the gable end of the dovecote was in danger of collapse due to a decayed interior tie-beam, and the repairs necessitated taking down the wall and rebuilding it. It is unfortunate that this process meant that the pigeon holes, i.e. pigeon nests formed in the interior brickwork, were destroyed. Internal improvements with wall board have covered up the nests on the other walls.

The Rectory, Tithe Barn, Dovecote and Village Cross are included in a list of buildings of special architectural or historic interest by the Town and Country Planning Acts.

The Almshouses

Jacinth Sacheverell, Lord of the Manor of Morley, left provision in his Will that his wife Elizabeth should erect 'an hosptial on Morley Moor for the habitation of six poor, lame or impotent men'. Elizabeth died a few months after her husband in 1656 but arranged for the work to be carried out, and the almshouses bear the date 1656 although they were not in fact built until later.

The Almshouses consist of six dwellings under one roof, each containing two rooms and there are gardens in front. A report made by the Charities Survey in 1826 states that 'the almshouses were all in good condition having been repaired about eight years previously. Three of the almshouses are appropriated to Morley and three to Smalley and three almsmen are appointed from each township. The Smalley almshouses had not been used by the almsmen for many years but were held by the Overseer of Morley for the use of parish paupers - the Overseer paying a rent of £2 a year for each tenement'.

Several improvements were made towards the end of the nineteenth century, and though no records can be traced it is thought that they included the retiling of the roof and alterations to the old open fireplaces, which were built up and oven and boiler type firegrates installed.

In 1937 repairs and improvements were made, the money being raised by voluntary subscription. These included stripping the roof and renewing defective timbers and laths, then retiling using the old tiles as far as possible. The outer doors were renewed or reconditioned in oak and leaded glazing put into the front windows. Dormer windows were put into the bedrooms, previously the only light that penetrated was from the room below. Alterations were made to the stairs - originally they consisted of open 'loft-type' steps without handrail, which lead directly up into the bedroom which was just an open platform or balcony, so presumably the 'lame' of the original bequest lived completely downstairs. This was typical cottage or even yeoman house building of the seventeenth century but of course such houses were usually extensively altered before the 1900's.

New floors were put into some of the houses

and sinks with water taps installed. Before that time water had been brought to stand pipes outside (probably when the Derwent Valley water came through), and prior to that water had to be carried from the pump at Priory Lodge or from Church Lane.

The almshouses were again renovated in 1974/5. The six dwellings were made into four, and electric central heating installed. Two of the almshouses are appropriated to Morley and two for Smalley. The qualification of almspeople states that they shall be poor persons either widow or widower or married couples of pensionable age, and may be required to contribute a weekly sum towards the cost of maintaining the almshouses.

The Croft

This stone built house on Morley Moor probably dates from as far back as the Almshouses. It consists basically of a main room downstairs with a kitchen attached, and the upstairs would have been very like the loft-type described in the almshouses. The stone mullions of the windows and the strength and solidity of the whole building still suggest, in spite of modernisations, the type of small yeoman houses that must have been common in eighteenth century Morley.

Old Morley Hall

Near the west end of the churchyard are the ruins of an old ancient gateway said to have been the entrance to the court of an ancient Hall, apparently of large dimensions, home of the Stathums and Sacheverells (Lords of Morley and Smalley), and the foundations of the building may still be traced in the adjoining field. The Hall was said to be connected to the church by a secret passage.

This arched gateway used to be known as the 'loaf-gate', a name thought to have survived from the days when John Stathum distributed bread to the poor. One of the memorial brasses in the church to John Stathum who died in 1435 gives details of the gifts he made to the church and also records that he gifted bread to the parish.

Sir William Dugdale in his 'Visitation of Derbys 1660' describes the coats of arms then existing in the windows of the old Hall, and the Reverend Charles Kerry[16] lists these in some detail in his copy of the Morley Registers.

No records can be traced to verify when the Hall was dismantled but the Reverend Charles Kerry writes that 'Jane Sacheverell is thought to have taken it down about 1750 (which accounts for the removal of the Sacheverell portraits to Renishaw)'. Jane Sacheverell however died in 1746. One of the Derbyshire Directories[17] states that it was still inhabited in 1755.

Edward Sacheverell Wilmot Sitwell who succeeded to the estates in 1772 shortly afterwards bought Stainsby Hall at Smalley and resided there with his family, and the Reverend Charles Kerry comments 'About the year 1839 a lawyer was employed to 'look over' a large collection of records and muniments at Stainsby belonging to the Wilmot Sitwell family, descendants of the ancient lords of Morley and Smalley, with the result that at least 'two large cartloads of them' comprising all the earliest (and to that gentleman the least legible) documents were committed to the flames. There can be no doubt that many of the old Sacheverell writings (now so scarce) perished in this grievous act of vandalism.

Morley Hall

The present Hall is situated in the field

- 23 -

adjacent to the church near to the site of the Old Hall above. It was built in 1837 by Mr. Sitwell.

Morley Manor

The Manor was erected early this century near to the Smalley boundary by Mrs. Sacheverell Bateman, and is built in the tudor style after the designs by Thomas Bodley Esq.,A.R.A. one of the most distinguished architects of our time. An artistic stone Pergola walk was designed by Sir Edward Lutyens. The stone for the house is reputed to have come from Wales.

In 1914 the house was used for a time as a hospital for the wounded, and in 1938 it was sold, together with other parts of the estate. This was bought by the Fitzwalter Wright family. In 1957 it was acquired by the Dr. Barnardo's organisation to be used as a home for children and is still used for this purpose today.

The Mausoleum

In the churchyard are the nineteenth century railed vault of the Sitwell family, also the Bateman mausoleum bearing their arms (three stars and three crescents) above the entrance.

Brackley Gate

This part of the district had thriving quarries in the eighteenth and nineteenth centuries, and across the last field where Quarry Head used to be a pair of stone cottages can be seen. These are now used as pigsties but were inhabited as late as 1930. They were mason built of stones which are more or less uniform in size and shape. The corners are well squared with square chimneys and the roof timbers suggest a craftsman's work.

Also in this area is an unusually shaped extension of the parish. To the right of the Horsley road across two fields are the remains of Moat Farm. This farm and the strip of land the width of a cart track which connected it to the road, paid tithe to Morley Church.

The 'Three Horse Shoes'

The 'Smithy' in Morley did double duty as both smithy and inn during the eighteenth century, when there are frequent accounts in the records of the Morley Constable for payments for ale or for travellers' lodgings.

It was run then by Robert King whose wife was the daughter of Samuel and Betty Kerry who owned the Rose and Crown at Smalley. The Reverend Kerry in his notes states that Robert was blind, and he describes Betty as 'a short roundabout woman with her hair done up in a roll and a mob cap on the top'. She died in 1831 at the age of 79.

Photographs taken at the beginning of this century show the Three Horse Shoes with thatched roof and the brewhouse on the right. Three steps led down into the cellar. The original cellars remain but the inn was dismantled and completely rebuilt in 1914.

Broomfield Hall

Earliest records available reveal that Broomfield Estate, containing 107 acres, was sold by the Executors of the late Sir Hugh Bateman in 1855 to Mr. Henry Boden who disposed of it to the late Robert Smith Esq., from whose Executors it was purchased by Charles Edward Schwind, Esq., J.P. in 1870.

Charles Schwind had Broomfield Hall itself

erected that year as his residence. By 1880, the grounds were tastefully laid out, and the Hall was lit by electricity. The estate also had a gas works complete with gasometer in what is now called 'Gas Yard' copse, just north of the main entrance and lodge. There was also a good water supply by that time on the estate.

By 1908 Lionel Schwind, Esq., occupied the Hall and was listed as a 'principal landowner', but by 1922 it was in the possession of George William Crompton, Esq., J.P., having been conveyed to him by a deed of 1st August 1914. G.W. Crompton, Esq., J.P., was still in possession of the property in 1933 and in 1944.

The Ordnance Survey Map of 1880 - first edition - shows that the Hall and Annexe, the grounds, paths, walled gardens, sunken gardens, and even the field boundaries and water troughs, were almost exactly as they remain today. Broomfield Cottages, 1,2,3 and 4, are also shown on the map with the milepost just south of them marked as it is today. The farm opposite them, however, was called 'Drapers' Hall' in 1880, but is given its present name 'Lime Farm' on the 1914 edition of the map.

In 1947 Broomfield Hall was purchased by the Derbyshire County Council.

CHAPTER 3

THE PARISH RECORDS

It is from the parish records that we found much of the history of Morley in the eighteenth and nineteenth centuries. Among the documents are records of the work of the churchwardens, the Overseer of the Poor, the Constable and of the Overseer of the Highways. The parish was made the administrative centre for local affairs in the Tudor period, but in Morley there are few records before the eighteenth century, and the fullest records are those covering the years when Robert Wilmot was rector.

Appointments were made in Morley of people, usually men but occasionally women, who were landowners or people of some standing who had to take their turn for a year in doing these various duties. They had to go to Derby to be sworn in by the appropriate County officials, and they were responsible for carrying out the law of the land in so far as it affected the parishioners of Morley. They were paid their expenses but otherwise there was no payment, and although they had to do their duties for only a year many of these posts involved their holders in a lot of work. It was in a way, government on the cheap, but in small communities such as Morley it must have meant that many people were actively involved in the affairs of the parish, and from their turn in office got a taste of the problems and difficulties of administration.

Today only the churchwardens still carry out duties in the parish. The roads passed in part to the Turnpike Trust and then at the end of the last century to the County; the Constable eventually became a paid and full-time member of the police force; and the care of the poor was taken over by the workhouses and then by the National Assistance Board. The old system would never work in large communities, but it is very interesting to look back and see a parish running its own affairs, and being responsible for its own well-being.

The Churchwardens' Accounts

In some places churchwardens' accounts exist from the middle of the sixteenth century, but in Morley the first mention of churchwardens is in 1647 when Wm. Bennett the Rector died and the various books belonging to the church - 'a Bible Jewell's Apology, a Psalme Book and also one Quushion, one carpett, one linen tablecloth marked with M.C. and an Erasmus Paraphrase' were handed over to Henry Hibbert, churchwarden, for safe keeping.

The churchwardens' accounts themselves start with 'Seth Brentnall his accompts, being churchwarden Anno 1711' but they were not kept regularly in any great detail until the nineteenth century. There are two officers, one of the people's warden who was appointed annually, and the other the rector's warden. Through much of the eighteenth century this latter post was held by a Brentnall, and in the latter part of the century and also in the nineteenth Thomas and then Robert Stainsby take over. The churchwardens were responsible for the general moral standard of the parish, and they had to ensure that the rector carried out his duties and that any ecclesiastical laws that the state made were enforced. It was the duty of these officers to check that everyone attended church and to inform the local J.Ps if there were absentees. The Derbyshire record of Presentments however, has no mention of any non-attendance in Morley. Churchwardens were also responsible for the upkeep of the fabric of the church, the apportionment of seats, the provision of fittings, the leasing of church lands and the administration of charities. To carry out these duties they could levy a church rate on all the landowners of the parish. (These church dues had to be paid until this century when they were ended because of opposition from people who were not members of the Church of England.)

One duty that was carried out was the result of a law ordering all churches to ring their bells on Sundays and on important occasions so a recurring expense was payments to ringers:-

1711	Paid the ringers for Nov. 5th	1s 6d
1756	" " " " " "	3s 6d
1757	" " " " New Year's Day	2s 6d
	" " " " ye King's birthday	2s 6d
(and also in that year 'spent at ye Smithy on ye King of Prushias birthday')		3s 0d

By 1811 the ringers' pay had gone up to six shillings, and in 1839 they received ten shillings for ringing for Queen Victoria's Coronation.

In 1789 the accounts show a typical year's work:-

June	Pd. Bread and Wine	4s 8d
July 4th	Pd. the Archdeacon's fee at the visitation	6s 8d
	Pd. with the breefs	1s 6d
	Pd. the paietor	2s 0d
	my jorne and expenses*	1s 6d
12th	Pd. to Mr. Hareson for mending clock wite	1s 0d
	Pd. for oile clock and the bells	1s 0d
Oct. 17th	Bread and Wine	4s 8d
	Pd. the visitation fees	4s 10d
	Pd. with the breaf	1s 0d
	my jorne and expenses*	1s 3d
Dec. 25th	Pd. Bread and Wine	4s 10d
Mar. 23rd	" " " "	4s 8d
	for 2 new bottes	8d
	for packing the same	1s 0d
	for washing the sarpes	4s 0d
	for thred and mending	4d
	for loucking the clock and clening	13s 0d

Mr. Talers Bill	1s 1½d
The ringers the year	6s 0d
for macking the Lave and counts	1s 6d

(*they had to go to Derby to be sworn in for the year by the Archdeacon.)

Some things however were not mentioned in the accounts. The Reverend Charles Kerry in the History of Smalley writes 'the late Mr. Whittaker the distinguished botanist of Ferriby Brook House informed me that a Black Letter Bible formerly belonging to Morley Church was said to be in the possession of Mr. Moses Smith of Allestree, and that there was a memorandum on the cover that the book was sold by the churchwardens of Morley to defray the expenses of a parish bull-baiting'.

The nineteenth century marked a time when churches were being put in repair and modernised and the churchwardens' accounts became much larger in consequence. New laws were passed too about the books in which births, the banns of marriage and the record of burials had to be kept, and every parish had to buy these books and also an iron chest in which to store them safely. In 1813 Morley bought one (still in the church) for £4.4s.0d., and the marriage register in 1823 cost 7s.6d. In 1811 the total expenses for the year came to nine pounds, and include a Prayer Book, the usual expenses for bread and wine, £1.14s.6d. for a new figures board, payments to the ringers and to the man who oiled and wound the clock, for washing the surplices, and for materials for the repair of the church. For the repairs they bought lime and hair, plaster stone and brick, and in that year too they paid for some of the stonework to be pointed. In 1815 it cost £2.19s.8d to clean the windows, and a bill for £23.19s.0d was presented by Wm. Cross for four new pews and the repair of others. 1816 was an expensive year:-

Feb.13th	Mr. Jn. Smith for painting and repairing windows	£ 9.17s.8d
	Saml. King's bill for ironwork	£ 3.13s.3d
	Mr. Thos. Dobbs bill for drawing whitewashing etc.	£12.12s.2d
	Mr. Jn. Weson for estimation and laths etc.	19s.0d

An alteration that took place about this time is recorded by Mr. T. Osborne Bateman in the Reliquary 1873. 'The Rev. Mr. Fox (who died in 1870) told me that the old people in the village remembered a rather handsome but decayed wooden screen which separated the chancel and the nave, and which had disappeared about fifty or sixty years before and of which there is now no trace. It was not thought well of by the then rulers of the church and it was sold to a farmer in the village for a guinea or so to serve for a hen-roost or some such other agricultural purpose'.

In 1822 the church was heated by two stoves costing some £9. and typically the expenses of having them installed is followed by the entry 'for ale' 1s.9d. These stoves than have to be cleaned and coal bought, usually from Kilburn, which cost in 1848, with cartage and toll charges £1.1s.6d. In 1830 a curious entry refers to the bricking up of windows, but this probably is the doorway at the west end of the church high up in the north aisle, which had once been an entrance to a gallery used by the Sacheverells. In the same year the church wall was raised at the considerable cost of £25.3s.7d. but which wall this was is not made clear. Perhaps it refers to the wall at the roadside since the ground is so much lower than the ground on which the church stands.

There is no reference in the accounts to the lease of church land, though during Robert Wilmot's time there are references to this in general vestry meetings. Only in 1802 do we see the Church as a landowner when there is:-

```
Lacey for cows Bulling                  14s.0d
Pd. Jn. Lacey for 4 cows bulin each      8s.0d
```

The administration of the charities, another of the churchwardens' duties was actually carried out by the Rector and the Vestry and the accounts appear in the Town Book.

A restoration of the church took place in 1850 and these are also listed by Mr. T. Osborne Bateman. 'Many of the monuments which are of alabaster were repaired, painted and restored at a cost of about £30. shared between the families of Pole, Wilmot, Sitwell and myself'.

'The old stained glass was in a most dilapidated condition and up to the time when Mr. S. Fox entered on his curacy about 1829 it was the custom of the friends and visitors at the village at times of hospitality such as Christmas and the Wakes, to show their regard for the church and its interesting objects, by pulling a bit of stained glass out of the windows to take home as a relic'.

The old windows and stained glass were restored in 1850 by W. Warrington of London. Mr. F. S. Ogden reports that a roll of 'cartoons' (one or two of them coloured) still exists, which appear to be of some of the windows as they were before the restoration. Mr. T. Osborne Bateman mentions several inaccuracies in the "History of Morley" by Samuel Fox relating to the inscriptions in the stained glass. He also has an interesting story to tell about one of the windows. 'Mr. Fox in his book describes a 'cross' as occupying part of a light in the East window of the South aisle. Mr. Warrington when he was superintending these restorations said this was some of the very oldest glass in the church. It is made of floreated fragments of a very peculiar character. One of Mr. Warrington's workmen had laid his hand on them, and because they were not connected with the picture glass, he said he thought he might keep them as a relic. When I saw them in London and the use he had turned them to by making this singular and elaborate piece of work somewhat resembling a cross, I insisted on paying the value of the workmanship and returning it thus made up, as an additional and legitimate object of interest in Morley Church'. Mr. Osborne Bateman gives the cost of the restoration of the windows as a guide to anyone engaged in similar works. 'The entire quantity of glass releaded, refixed, repaired and somewhat augmented was measured at 185 feet according to the workman's peculiar way of measuring. Mr. Warrington's original estimate to make a good job of this was one hundred pounds, but when on completion he told me that two hundred pounds would barely remunerate him, I paid him the money without objection so highly was I satisfied with the result!'

The Gazeteer and Journal of Derbyshire[18] by Francis White also records the restoration that took place at the church in 1850 and particularly mentions that the old pews were worked up into the present open pews, and the spire was heightened 2 feet 7 inches (thus making the height of the tower and spire 113 feet). The whole restoration was done at an expense of £426 raised by subscriptions.

Church Music

There were regular payments 'to singers' in the nineteenth century and in 1807 fifteen shillings was paid 'for desks for the use of the singers'. Music was provided by a bassoon at one time and this can still be seen in Derby Museum with the following particulars. 'Used in Morley Church, Derbyshire about 1820. Presented by the late Mr. Shaw Allsop'. It is very probable that other instruments were used as well but no other record has survived.

Mr. T. Osborne Bateman throws some light on the arrangements in the church at the time.
'Previous to the year 1840 there was a singers gallery projecting into the church in front of the present tower arch, which was then filled up with lath and plaster. About that time Mr. Fox suggested to me to have this gallery set back and placed within the tower, the arch being opened. It was accordingly done at my expense, and was according to our then lights a great improvement, as the church was very short in proportion to its width. This improvement involved no great cost perhaps about thirty pounds. At the final restoration of the church in 1850 this gallery was taken down, and the singers were moved into the chancel, in accordance with the church arrangements now so generally better understood and practised.'

Canon K. H. MacDermott A.R.C.M. gives some very interesting facts in his book "The Old Church Gallery Minstrels".[19] ...'Many churches had their own bands which came into being soon after the Restoration and throve with variable fortune for about two hundred years, and there were keen musicians in nearly every village and town in England. The bands usually consisted of from three to eight players, half playing on stringed and the others on woodwind instruments. Minstrels usually performed in the gallery at the West end of the church, when there was no gallery the musicians performed in some convenient place in the nave, they rarely seem to have occupied the chancel. It was the custom for whole families for generations to serve in the choir or band: any member of a household who had failed to try to take part was regarded almost as an outcast. Not many children seem to have been employed in the old choirs, probably because the melodies of the hymn-tunes were sung by the tenor voices down to about 1850, the treble part being rendered by women. It is well perhaps that the old choirmen were satisfied as a rule with their own performance, for very few writers on the subject of church music in the past ever had much praise for them, and scathing criticisms of both the singing and playing are frequent in the books of the period. Thomas Mace in "Music's Monument" (1676) in allusion to the psalm singing of the day says 'It is sad to hear what whining, yelling and screeching there is in many congregations, as if the people were affrighted or distracted. Dr. Burton in his Journal (1750) wrote - 'They sing psalms by preference not set to the old and simple tunes, but as if in a tragic chorus, changing about in strophe and anti-strophe and stanzas with good measure, but yet there is something offensive to my ear when they bellow to excess and bleat out some goatish noise with all their might.'

The 'musickers' were often ignorant, somewhat without musical talent, frequently poor executants and generally somewhat irreverent, but always full of zeal in matters musical. They practised singing several nights a week at home or in church; or they learned their instruments slowly and laboriously, often without any tuition save that afforded by an instruction book or a fellow player. Many a young fellow who had little 'schooling' would learn some instrument with unflagging earnestness and laboriously copy out his music; the cost of printed books being far beyond the reach of his slender means.

The privilege of occupying a seat in the gallery was most jealously guarded, and ordinary non-musical members of the congregation were not allowed 'up among the gods', and sitting in the minstrels gallery was obviously reserved for the few. Apparently the singers were encouraged to regard themselves as among the elect in the musical portion of the service, at whose feet the ordinary members of the congregation had to sit and humbly learn!

There can be little doubt that the singing in the olden days was more lusty than refined, more original than artistic, more vigorous than tuneful; but the whole-hearted efforts of the devoted musicians largely made up for a lack of knowledge and skill. There was a simple directness about their voluntary labours which makes one regret the bygone days.

In 1850 the church was presented with a Harmonium by Mrs. Sitwell of Morley Hall. This was later transferred to the school and was in constant use for many years by the day school and for Sunday School hymn singing.

The present organ was installed beneath the south chancel arch in 1885 and was removed to its present position in the tower arch in 1952. The choir stalls were installed in 1884 and were a great improvement to the former simple benches.

CHAPTER 4

POOR RELIEF IN MORLEY

As in the case of the Constable and the Overseer of the Highways someone had to be found each year to undertake the post of Overseer of the Poor. It was not a popular job since it took quite a lot of time and was unpaid, and so a rota of those eligible was made, and women if they owned land had to serve their turn just as did the other landowners. Mary Alsop was Morley Overseer of the Poor for a year in the 1790s. Sometimes a parish might hire an overseer, but Morley in 1788 decided that this should not be done until everyone who was eligible for duty had served their turn.

Each parish was responsible for everyone born in it or who had been settled there for over a year, unless the Overseer had applied to their native parish to determine that if they needed help their original parish would accept the responsibility. It was because of this system that each parish tried to keep out new settlers and to keep paupers on the move back to their home parish. The money came from a rate levied each year by the Overseer in committee with the parish vestry, and a popular Overseer was one of course who kept the rates down. In 1788 the levy in Morley was one shilling in the pound of rateable value, but in the following year was only fourpence. In England as a whole however rates were rising rapidly in the eighteenth century from one million pounds in the 1750s to ten million pounds in the 1800s. This was the major reason why 1833 saw the start of the notorious workhouse system.

Poor relief wasn't all of an Oliver Twist nature however. Morley was a small parish, only some forty-eight families were listed in the 1801 census, and everyone must have known everyone else and have known their opportunities and their difficulties. When in 1800 Thomas Smith was thrown into jail at Lenton in Notts. the vestry decided 'the said Pauper's family is to be immediately brought home to Morley' and the words 'home to Morley' have a welcoming ring to them.

The principles on which poor relief were given in Morley were the same as those generally current in England as a whole. In 1780 they were set in the minutes of a vestry meeting:-

(1) No new settlers were to be admitted unless they brought a certificate from their last place of legal settlement accepting responsibility for them if they became paupers. For example Morley itself sent an acknowledgement to Brailsford in 1779 that Samuel Slater belonged to Morley parish. It was this principle that made the growth of industries so difficult since it prevented new labour coming in. In 1800 the Reverend Mr. Wilmot opposes a suggestion for a factory in Morley 'a building by Godfrey Turner ... liable to be detrimental by introducing into Morley a stocking manufactory with its certain attendant ills by increasing the poor rate'.

(2) Those settlers without a certificate were to be removed.

Some of those who lived on the common had no legal right either to land or to residence in Morley. There was too the curious case of a man who claimed assistance for his children, but rumours must have been rife for the vestry decided to 'inquire into the truth of his being legally married to the woman he now calls his wife'. They were right to do so for 'she was the wife of another man, he purchased her from him'. The children consequently were the responsibility of the woman's home parish, and not Morley.

(3) Men who were the putative fathers of illegitimate children were required to pay maintenance for the woman and her child if they were in any position to do so. Quite large sums (thirty pounds spread over three to seven years) were demanded on several occasions. If the father was unable to support the child then the parish could be required to do so. Chaddesden for instance applied to Morley's Overseer for the maintenance for a child of Elizabeth Lands.

(4) Able-bodied poor were to be sent 'on the rounds' which meant that they went to each ratepayer in turn and had to

do whatever work was given them. They were to be allowed sixpence a day and their keep. In 1744 Joseph Sandey 'did consent to have his two lesser children put out and is allowed two shillings per week and is to be employed as follows' and a list of the ratepayers was then given. Fifty years later Hansley who applied for relief was sent on the rounds and allowed five shillings a week for his family. William Chambers however, had his relief stopped in the spring on the grounds that 'he should now be able to make money from brickmaking as the season begins'. Perhaps the season wasn't very good though since in the June the Parish provided money to buy him a bed.

(5) Women who were able to work were provided with tow for spinning as were Mary Longman and Olive Fletcher's daughter in 1795.

(6) Children were to be apprenticed out. In 1796 the Overseer of the Poor was instructed 'to inquire for a situation to apprentice Samuel Stansby's unfortunate son to a stocking needlemaker'. They must have been unsuccessful however for in 1799 he was sent to Crich Workhouse 'as the most human act that can be done for him, there being a school close to the Workhouse where he may get instruction sufficiently to enable him to get his livelihood as a country schoolmaster, and thereby be rendered a useful member of society, and be freed from the most intolerable burden a man can possibly bear - that of ignorance accompanied with idleness'.

The girls were not so fortunate. 'Female children who are able to perform any work are to be sent for a year to each inhabitant (ratepayer) of Morley and clothed at the Parish expense'. Life must have seemed very hard to these unhappy drably clothed little drudges.

These principles may not however have been applied strictly according to the letter, and indeed in the accounts there seems to have been far more real help given than insistence on the letter of the law.

```
1787 Poor Account:-
May 12th   Slater for medicines            2s. 0d
    13th   Wm. Bailey for wooleys          6s. 0d
Jun.29th   Martin for childs cloth         2s. 0d
```

Jul. 9th	Burrow's children	3s. 6d
13th	A shirt for Slater	3s. 4½d
24th	A shirt for Longman	4s. 0d
30th	Thos. Smith ¾ rent	£1.10s. 0d
Aug.13th	Burrow's children	4s. 0d
Oct. 3rd	Burrow's children	3s. 0d
Dec.15th	Cloth for Slater's child	8s. 5d

1788

Jan 7th	3 prs. shoes and shirt	10s. 0d
8th	Sarah Oxley's coals	11s. 6d
23rd	Mary Roper's coals	5s. 0d
	drawing (N.B. tolls to be paid)	5s. 0d
Feb.26th	Tho. Martin	8s. 0d
	for mending the child's shoes	1s. 0d
Mar. 2nd	Longman	2s. 0d
11th	Burrows fatherless children	8s. 0d
29th	Longman	2s. 0d
24th	Shirts for Slater and Long	9s. 0d

These were only part of the accounts for one financial year which totalled nearly £46, and they do suggest a reasonably generous attitude on the part of the Vestry.

One of the problems Morley faced as they noted in 1789, was that in previous centuries money had been left for the poor, and these charities attracted people from other parishes who once they had established residence in Morley by working for a year, often below the average wage rate, would be able to benefit from the eleven or twelve pounds a year that was distributed. So it was laid down that this money was not to go 'to people who own a cow, house or land nor those receiving poor relief'. Robert Wilmot records with some naivety the reaction of one woman to this news. 'Widow Joyce Smedley has purchased land and built herself a house this last year and so become disqualified ... When I told her so she showed the greatest discontent and resentment towards myself and in her passion she declared that I should not have that plea to deprive her of the money another time, for that she would sell her house and land...' He continues, 'I think it would be a good idea to have the regulations for the distribution of the Charity money wrote upon a board and stuck up in the Church, as no person after that can claim a share of it if not entitled thereto, which will prevent much vexation and disappointment for themselves and do away with all ground for abuse of the distributors who ought always to be the Rector, the Churchwarden and the Overseer of the Poor'.

These charities derived their income from various pieces of land that had been left by charitable donors. There was land in Nun's Green in Derby, in Morley, in Ockbrook and in Leicestershire, and also the interest on £20. left for the poor. These charities can still be seen recorded on boards in the church.

There are records of two particularly interesting cases of poor relief in the late eighteenth century. One was that of William Hardy. He was not simply a labourer but a man of some small substance, he rented land on which he pastured a cow and his house had at least one mark of refinement about it for he possessed a clock. When Hardy fell ill he was unable to meet the rent for his land and applied to the Vestry for help. They obviously felt that he should be helped to keep some sort of independence and decided to advance him the money for the rent, instead of demanding that he sell his cow and maintain himself with that money. They did however, charge the Overseer 'to sell his clock which they judged to be an useless article, towards paying the money now wanted, and they agreed that his cow shall not be meddled with till it shall be seen whether he recovers'.

After a while 'Hardy was suspected of pretending sickness, as all the faculty who had been consulted respecting him declared they discovered no symptoms of ill-health'. The Vestry then decided to stop payments 'which had the desired effect, for he immediately became perfectly well tho' he had been supported by the Parish for two years under the idea of his being unable to work and for the last year and half had regular pay from the Overseer of the Poor - for two years past he sat constantly in the house and appeared always wrapped up about his head. The whole of his conduct appears extraordinary as he had a good character and had been esteemed a good and able labourer'.

In another case the Vestry ran into difficulties.

Mary Kerry of Smalley which was part of Morley parish, married Thomas Longman in 1780 and they obviously had to turn to the poor rates quite early in their married life, for the name turns up quite regularly in the accounts. In 1794 she was left a widow with two young children and had to depend completely on poor relief. The Vestry with its eye on the rates decided that Mary could do something towards her own support and instructed the Overseer to procure tow, another member of the Vestry had an old spinning wheel that could be put into running order, and Mary was to spin enough yarn to bring in the two or three shillings necessary for her own needs. Whether Mary felt that this was expecting too much of a woman for whom life had always been hard, or whether she genuinely suffered from ill-health we cannot at this distance say, but certainly the monthly minutes record with almost unfailing regularity that Mary had been unable to spin enough yarn and had therefore needed extra help.

The crisis came eventually. Perhaps the Overseer spoke harshly to an ill woman or perhaps Mary was inspired to get her own back on that governing body who she must have felt, had had it easy all their lives. Anyway Mary knew her rights. She walked to Derby to see the magtrate John Port dismissed the complaint without making any order thereon, and he declared he thought the complainant ought to have been punished. We are at any rate left in no doubt about the Vestry's reactions. The next entry in the monthly records covers the full page, and every downstroke of the pen is overflowing with righteous indignation. Here was a woman whom they had supported for years. Not merely supported but furnished with the comforts of coal, clothing bedding and food. Admittedly at that moment the bed clothes promised had not actually been delivered, but one can almost hear them declaring that nothing would persuade them to deliver them now. Mary Longman and the Vestry had been at loggerheads far too long for them to bear her presence any longer. The solution lay in their hands and the Rector Mr. Wilmot was instructed to put in hand negotiations for her immediate despatch to Crich Workhouse.

He first went to see the Workhouse and came back with a glowing report. 'He had arrived at the House at the instant that the Dinner was serving - Each inmate had a porringer of broth with bread in it and then a dish of excellent boiled mutton, a bit of bacon, plenty of good potatoes and a very large piece of bread. It was more than the generality of them consumed at once but was set aside by them for their four o' clock or afternooning. Two days in the week they have such hot meat dinners, and on two days cold meat and bread and cheese, the other days puddings, milk porridge, and their breakfast is milk porridge and their supper bread and cheese. The bedrooms were perfectly clean and sweet, and there was a sitting room for the women separate from the men. The paupers so far from complaining declared they had every comfort. Asked if they had plenty of food always they said yes, and one of them went so far as to say that they 'had not only plenty but that which was good, that indeed they lived upon the fat of the land'. A far cry this from Oliver Twist but it was still a bitter pill for Mary Longman, for her children were taken away from her. The elder daughter the Vestry decided was now of an age to go out to work and the younger one was taken in by one of the Vestry (incidentally he got almost as much for that one extra mouth as Mary had been receiving for all three of them).

Mary doesn't let things rest at that. No sooner had the Vestry despatched her to Crich with a universal sigh of relief of having rid themselves of a tiresome burden and yet having dealt like upright and just men, than Mary returned. She had walked out of the Workhouse and come back to plead to be allowed to settle in Morley again. Her case however was dismissed in a couple of lines, and she was sent back.

A year later though no more was officially recorded, her name reappears, not on the poor rate accounts, but on those of the charities, and for the next twenty years Widow Longman duly gets a share of Dame Goditha's Dole. Then at last she does vanish. No more charity receipts, no record of death and burial, no further record at all. Perhaps that elder daughter sent to work in 1799 was able to offer a home to her mother. We can only hope that some such happy ending came to round off the life of such a born rebel.

And, too, Mary Longman's story rounds off Morley's poor relief. A record of a group of people who had to find from themselves and their neighbours the money to help their own poor, and who did it not ungenerously.

CHAPTER 5
THE PARISH CONSTABLE

The constable, like the other officers was elected on a yearly basis. There was no property qualifications and the man appointed was usually a small freeholder or someone who followed some trade. He was responsible for maintaining law and order, and although serious cases had to be carried to a J.P. he could himself carry out some punishments such as beating vagrants or detaining in the lock-up. He had to see that no-one settled in the parish without permission, and that those travellers who had a pass to move to their legal parish were assisted on their journey. When a crime had been committed and a 'hue and cry' raised, it was the constable's job to assure himself that the man was not in his parish and to carry the hue and cry to the next parish.

There were also many administrative duties that were imposed on him by the government. There were various taxes such as the window tax. As early as 1702 the constable was noting on his accounts three shillings expenses for going in to Derby 'about ye window tax'. Several houses in Morley have bricked-in windows which suggest that as the tax grew heavier, householders tried this method of lessening their dues. Morley Hall, Morley House Farm and the Rectory all show such windows.

The army was recruited on a basis of so many men from each area being 'called up'. They were not named but the required number had to be found, and it was the constable of the parish who had to produce the 'volunteers'. Sometimes men could be hired and in 1794 the constable's accounts show the sum of £3.13s.0d. paid to 'a trand (trained) soulger'. In 1799 the constable goes on a 'Journey to Cotmanhay to fetch Harrison for ye militia' and in the same year (which is

- 45 -

the middle of the Napoleonic Wars) he goes round the parish with a list for the general defence. He had to keep lists of those who could be called on for army service, and these lists were sent to Derby regularly until well into the nineteenth century.

The duties of the constable included those of Pest Officer and there are many entries in the parish records referring to payments for the destruction of sparrows, hedgehogs and moles. A few coppers were paid for a hedgehog, and from 1825 to 1850 the yearly payments 'to Molecatcher' average nearly six pounds. The amount paid for birds, also for the quantity caught is given in the accounts for 1840:-

	Paid for birds at 1d each	£2.17s.0d
Oct.5th	" " 840 small birds at 1d	£1.15s.0d
	" " 32 score of birds 6d per score	16s.0d
	" " George Taylor for birds	11s.9d

There were other parish duties that fell to the constable and one that is frequently mentioned is mending gates. While Morley had a common on which all animals could be pastured these animals had to be prevented from straying. If they strayed within the parish they were caught and 'pinned' i.e. locked up in a pound, and the owner had to pay a fine to get them out. Brackley Gate and one at Morley Lime are mentioned and this must have been to prevent animals straying out of the parish. Details of building the Pinfold are given in the accounts:-

July 28th 1810

Thos. Seals bill for stone and building Pinfold	£4.1s.0d
Rbt. King's bill for ale, iron and lead	£1.2s.1d
One man one day filling stone	2s.6d
Gave the men for helping to load	1s.6d
Drawing stone 3 days	£1.4s.0d
Lime and fetching sand for do	4s.6d
Pd. Rbt. Allsopp for a gate	£1.0s.6d
A lock for same	10d
Our man a day for levelling the Pinfold	2s.6d

Morley Church (built in the 13th Centruy)

Toll Bar Cottage (demolished in 1929)

Broomfield Hall

Workmen at Morley Quarry (c. 1860)

There were too occasional domestic crises, for instance the constable's accounts for 1800 show a payment to Rbt. King at the Smithy Inn for lodging Samuel Slater when he and his wife were quarrelling. Occasionally too the constable would use the inn when holding men who were to go before the magistrates; Isaac Archer was served with a warrant in 1808 and two shillings was charged by the constable for stopping with him all night at the Smithy. He similarly attended Lark Wathall all night in 1810 and later in the year for two days and a night, but why Wathall needed these attentions is not clear. £3.5s.0d. was paid for a licence for him and a subsequent shilling for his examination at Smalley, so possibly the man was ill in some way and had a licence to beg. Poor travellers were lodged at the inn and Robert King was paid for this by the constable, and these travellers were themselves given money to continue their journeys. As early as 1699 the constable's accounts show small sums from twopence to a shilling 'given to travellers with a pass' and on one occasion sixpence was paid to 'carrying a cripple to Breadsall'.

Crime seems to have come rarely to Morley. The method of catching criminals by the hue and cry seems very crude and inadequate and indeed in the only important case of trouble in Morley, it was not used as far as we can see by the records. The report in fact comes from the 'Derby Mercury' of 1781. The Rector Robert Wilmot had an advertisement put in regarding William Lee who 'is charged with a violent suspicion of having robbed the church at Morley... Whoever will apprehend him and lodge him in any of His Majesty's Gaols of this Kingdom shall receive five guineas reward from the Rev. Mr. Wilmot; and in case he is convicted they will be entitled to £40. more'. Nothing of this is mentioned in Morley's parish records and how William Lee was suspected is unknown, but their suspicions were correct for he was captured 'at a Publick House in this Town (Derby) where he had just called in for a Pot of Ale' and the silver chalice cup and large pewter tankard which he had stolen were recovered from the sand bank at Nottingham where he had hidden them. Lee was tried at the next Assizes, found guilty and sentenced to death (the normal punishment for stealing any article worth more than five shillings) but he was later reprieved. From the bill for the prosecution it appears this affair cost the parish £20.17s.1d. Forty Pounds was allowed by Act of Parliament as reward for detection of culprit which was paid by the under sheriff.

The Reverend Charles Kerry writes 'Tradition says that Lee obtained entrance to the church by breaking the painted window immediately over the recumbent effigy of Katherine Babington when the nose and finger ends of the figure were broken off by the unscrupulous visitor'. He also states that the silver chalice cup given to the church by Elizabeth Sacheverell was still in use at Morley in 1902.

Apart from crime there were other points the constable had to attend to. Everyone had to pay a levy for the expenses incurred by the constable and moneys had to be paid to the County for 'Houses of Correction, board of prisoners, marshalls, a country gaoler and also country bridges'. This levy was the constable's responsibility. He had also to present lists of Jurors to the Derby magistrates and lists of assessments for any taxes.

It was not all hard work however, for there are also fairly regular entries in the accounts of 'paid to parish meeting' and in 1841 a more specific 'paid for Beef at parish meeting 8s.0d. and for ale at same 13s.0d.', and by 1862 the account for ale at one of these meetings reached the sum of nineteen shillings. It is hardly surprising that the levy for all that the constable had to do reached two shillings in the pound at times in the nineteenth century.

CHAPTER 6
ROADS

The whole problem of road building was shirked during the Middle Ages, and it was not until industries began to develop in the eighteenth century that the necessity for improving the roads compelled some reforms. Throughout the period 1600 to the late 1800s each parish was responsible for the upkeep of roads in their own district, and so there was one more job that was annually laid on the shoulders of one of the villagers. Everyone in the village had to help with road repairs and the Overseer of the Highways had to organise this and see it was done properly. Labourers had to work four to six days a year doing unpaid statute labour; landowners had to supply teams - horse and cart and two men for four days a year. Often in Morley there was also a levy which paid for materials and implements. If the Overseer was a weak man or busy on his own affairs little was done. On one occasion at least however, an enthusiastic and active Overseer was appointed but this was unusual enough for the Vestry to record its vote of thanks for 'his particular attention to and spirited amendment of the roads in the parish last year' (1773).

The Reverend Robert Wilmot seems to have managed to encourage attention to the roads for in 1792 he writes with pride 'the highways are nearly all put in good repair... In 1777 the bye-roads were almost all of them impassable in the winter for carts and waggons, now there is not in the whole Township more than 200 yards of road that a chaise cannot pass on at any time of the year'.

A list of the tools owned by the Overseer of the Highways in 1788 consisted of one large hammer, one cavil, and two hacks. Some of the entries in the Highway accounts give a picture of the type of work done.

1789	Pd. for materials and labour -	
	120 loads stone @ 4d per load	£2. 0s. 0d
	60 " " @ 5d " "	£1. 5s. 0d
	hacked in the roads thro' the parish	£1. 1s. 0d
	4 days widening the lane	6s. 0d
	John Turner throwing up the road	£1.12s. 0d
	J.Roome 42 days work & getting sand for covering	£2.16s. 0d
	Pd. to last surveyor to balance his acct.	£5. 9s. 3d
	Pd. to surveyor of the Turnpike Rd.	£4.14s. 0d
	Pd. Sml.Slater opening the water course on the moor	3s.10d
1794	Isaac Fisher's bill for 6 Guide posts	£4.11s. 0d
	John Rotherham's Bill for writing Guide Posts	£2.12s. 6d
1795	for levelling and sofing* in the Lime Lane	£2. 5s. 0d
	two wiskets	1s. 0d
1798	Starbuck repairing Moor Gate wall	1s. 6d
	Bonnington " " " "	1s. 6d
	Scouring moor ditch	4s. 6d
1799	Hacking in Toad Lane	7s. 0d
	" " Moor Lane	7s. 0d
	Laying a causeway in Toad Lane	5s.10d
1806	Repairing bridge at Ferreby Brook	1s. 0d
	A new riddle	3s. 6d
	2 shovels	7s. 0d
1822	clearing out the brook in Potters Lane	1s. 6d
	Cash to Mrs.Sam'l King for ale for statute duty	£1. 4s. 8d
	Mr.Sam'l King's bill for repairing Hacks Hammers	£1.15s. 8d
	Mr.Green for hack helves and new male	17s. 7d
1823	Thatch & thatching John Kerry's house (the toll house)	3s. 6d
1824	lock for Pound Gate (enclosure for stray animals)	1s. 0d
1829	more thatch for Kerry's house	£1. 1s. 0d

(* sough - ditch or drain)

The Turnpike Road

An industrial country needs a good network of communications - road, river and canal, and rail. This need became increasingly obvious as the Industrial Revolution gathered force in the eighteenth century. Morley's interest in canal developments was limited to the Little Eaton canal which carried the stone brought down to it from the quarries near Brackley Gate. The railway line skirts the boundary of the parish and played no part in Morley's history. The roads however, were not left solely in the care of the Overseer of the Highways.

In 1764 a group of men prominent in the country came together for the purpose of forming a Turnpike Trust Commission to organise the road from Derby to Mansfield. They had an Act of Parliament passed enabling them to make a good road over this stretch and to recompense themselves for their capital outlay by charging tolls. They hired a surveyor (James Wilder) who was the skilled man in charge of the whole road, and who saw that the various contractors carried out their work effectively. Richard Beresford, for instance, contracted 'to make a substantial good road from Smalley Common one mile on Morley Lane towards Derby' for 2/9d a yard and Anthony Turton of Ripley did the same from 'Ferribay Brook to Vincent Fisher's in Morley' for 2/-d. a yard. This was to be a road 18 feet wide with a surface of at least 15" - 18" of gravel or stone and the hedges to be cut back.

Toll gates were put up at Little Chester and Smalley. For some years 1766 - 1786 there was considerable disagreement about whether a subsidiary gate or chain should be put up at the Smithy at Morley. Decisions on matters like these were made at the meetings the Commissioners held every few weeks. (Their minute books are to be found in the County Archives at Matlock). Reading the minutes is almost like watching a jack-in-the-box:-

June 1765 'A gate to be immediately erected on the side of the Turnpike Road ... at the Smithy Shop in Morley Liberty leading from Morley to Morleymoor'.

Aug. 1765 The gate at Morley to be taken down as 'the continuing of the gates will not answer the purposes of the act'.

Aug. 1766 John Gregg to take over the care of the Turnpike Gate at Morley at a wage of 6/- a week.

Dec. 1766 John Gregg to take over the Toll House at Smalley; the chains at Morley to be immediately taken down.

Apr. 1767 Chain to be immediately put across Turnpike at Morley and Thomas Slack of Horsley Park to collect the toll.

Oct. 1767 The chain at Morley Smithy to be taken down and discontinued.

And so it went on. By 1779 however, they had at least a house for when the chain was ordered to be taken down, on that occasion Samuel Martin the collector was 'to quit and deliver up the possession of the house in which he now dwells, erected by order of the said Commissioners near the said chain'.

When the chain was up at Morley half toll was taken there and half at Smalley. There is no direct evidence but it does seem possible that it was rivalry between Smalley and Morley for the money to be gained that led to this disagreement. After 1785 the Commissioners ended their policy of appointing and paying toll-keepers themselves, and instead the various gates were offered each year to the highest bidder. Obviously the Commissioners wanted the maximum number of gates since this was their sole source of income and consequently Morley's gate is never again disturbed. It was let at sums varying from £114. in 1785 to as much as £300. in the 1830s.

Through Morley's gate a lot of coal was carted from the collieries at Smalley and Mapperley. There were stringent regulations about the weight of loads and too the width of the wheels on these heavy wagons was prescribed at 'not less than 9" x 2"'. The Commissioners were careful to follow up reports of and to exact fines for these offences. A weighing machine was set up at Morley in 1787. Traffic within the village did not have to pay tolls of course but the cost of goods coming to the village did rise. The Overseer of the Poor in his accounts records the tolls on a cartload of coal as 1/- and the cost of transport as only 6d.

The Turnpike Trust claimed a proportion of the Statute Labour work as it was maintaining one of the roads through the parish. In 1765 Isaac Brentnall, sometime Morley Overseer of the Highways received 7/- a week for organising this work in Morley, Smalley and Breadsall. He was dismissed in 1767 but they must have had trouble without him for in 1770 there are threats of prosecution if the Statute work is not done.

Macadam was one of the great road-builders of the nineteenth century and of course it is his name that has been used to describe tarmac or macadamized roads. In 1825 the Commissioners decided 'to avail themselves of Mr. Macadam's attendance at Derby' and in 1826 he was employed by them on the Derby - Mansfield Road.

Tolls continued to be collected throughout most of the nineteenth century. Mr. Tomlinson took over the Morley Gate as late as 1872 although officially all roads were to be cared for by groups of parishes financed by a highways rate after 1862. England's turnpike roads had once been the envy of all Europe, but the record of complaints in the minutes of the Derby - Mansfield turnpike show how poorly these roads were maintained by the middle of the nineteenth century. Breadsall Hill in particular was so dangerous on account of the potholes (three feet in diameter and up to eighteen inches deep) and boulders in the middle of the road, that a carrier sued the Trust for £20. in 1872 - £15. for his horse which died from its injuries and £5. for damage to his cart. The money put up a century before for the purpose of improving the roads had become simply an investment which paid half yearly dividends to their heirs. The Trust was eventually wound up in 1875, and the Toll Gate House put up for sale was bought for £100 by Mr. Robert Sitwell. Originally there was only one door to this building facing on to the Mansfield Road. Set into the wall on the other side of the door were the rings into which the chains were hooked when stretched across the road during the period of the payment of the tolls. Mr. Robert Leeson, who was the owner from 1903, built another room on to the north-east side of the building, thereby making a second entrance. It was demolished in September 1929 to make way for the widening of the road. The blocks of quarried stone from which it was built were later used to build a bungalow a few metres further along the Mansfield Road to the north-east. The original roof slates and three of the window frames were also used for the new building. Behind the Toll Bar Cottage property on a small strip of land is a public well. This was formerly used by most of the houses around as it was the nearest source of drinking water.

CHAPTER 7

THE REVEREND ROBERT WILMOT

Robert Wilmot was inducted as Rector of Morley on the 23rd December 1777 at the age of twenty-seven. His father, Richard Wilmot, was a former Rector of Morley as well as a Canon of Windsor and Vicar of Mickleover, and his uncle Sir Edward Wilmot was physician to both George II and III. They were sons of Joyce Sacheverell who was a co-heiress of the Sacheverell estates and who married Robert Wilmot of Chaddesden. He was therefore, well connected in the county and in a position to know something of the affairs of court.

During his incumbency at Morley, George III suffered increasingly from mental disorders that left England without firm leadership. Abroad the French Revolution followed the path of increasing violence which led to the long war between France and England.

Robert Wilmot makes his comments on these issues and with our knowledge of what was to happen it is impossible not ot be impressed by his foresight. But in the main he gave his energies to the running of the parish, and it is due to him that we have such a vivid picture of the Morley of that time. Every parish record is full and accurately kept. There are the ordinary records of births, marriages and deaths - interspersed with Wilmot's own comments; there are minutes of Vestry meetings, the accounts of the Parish Constable, the Overseer of the Poor and the Overseer of the Highways; there is a census made by the clerk of the parish and another fuller one ordered by the government; the only thing lacking is a good map that would have made it possible to place exactly the houses and farms of those people whom we come to know so well from the records.

Extracts from the Reverend Mr. Wilmot's comments in the Registers

Weather is traditionally a subject that interests everyone in England, but it was not just interest but its vital importance in a village that depended almost completely on its farms that made Robert Wilmot write about it so often. A bad year could mean semi-starvation for the poor. For instance in 1783 corn was dear and the potato crop 'much used as a substitute for bread' was poor so that 'a scarcity and dearness with a bad quality obliged them (the poor) to reduce too much for health'.

and here is a full extract from 1799:-

'This year was in general very healthy, but from the Corn crops having been ill harvested, and the Wheat very soft and unsould I find Diarrhoea becoming very prevalent, and I much fear that there will shortly be much sickness. Till very late we had no Spring from the drought which prevailed, and the cold and frosty nights which continued till May there was but little vegetation; there was no grass for the cattle to be turned to till June, and a general distress prevailed for want of fodder. In Cheshire Hay was so scarce that a Guinea was given in some places for a Hundred weight.

In July the rain set in, and there was after that scarcely ever a dry day and straw could not be had at any price. Before the grass came in the Spring, they were so distressed for fodder for their cattle in the Hundred of Worral in Cheshire, that some of the farmers were under the necessity of giving their new calved cows their own milk as soon as drawn from them, in order to keep them alive. After the continued drought of some months the rain set in about the latter end of May, and from that time till the frost set in about Christmas we had never eight and forty hours together without wet - the Hay tho' not a bad crop was almost everywhere spoiled, the Corn crops in this part of England were drowned and starved - the consequence was a deficiency of grain when brought under the flail, and that unsound and bad, and which in consequence soon rose to the enormous price of One Guinea per strike Winchester - Beans sixteen shillings - Oats eight shillings - Barley nine shillings. I speak this of the first quality, inferior samples somewhat lower. New Wheat was from twelve to fourteen and all other grain proportionately dear. Meat was very cheap, fat sheep could not be sold for more than $3\frac{3}{4}$d. The poor begin to suffer very much, and I fear before another Harvest there is no chance of things being better.'

INDUSTRY

In the eighteenth century the Industrial Revolution began, and for the first time factories and industrial towns were to be seen. Men like Robert Wilmot watched this development with horror and concern. The American Revolution and the French Revolution seemed to develop from the opposition to authority that was to be found amongst these factory workers, and they foresaw riot and revolution in England.

In 1795, writing of that Thomas Chambers the stockinger who earned thirty-five shillings a week, Robert Wilmot observes...

> 'so ill do I think of manufacturers in general that if I wished to curse any people, I would introduce among them a manufactory, which would soon introduce every vice and depravity that human nature is capable of: - this is a shocking reflexion but experience evinces its truth, and whenever this Empire is overthrown it will be done by manufacturers - for among them the great seditionists have found the true soil for the culture of their diabolical principles'.

The French Revolution

In 1789 the Revolution started as a movement to introduce parliamentary government, but extremists soon took over and mass executions, usually by the guillotine, led to a Reign of Terror. In England it was widely feared that the workers in the industrial towns might take up the cry of 'Liberty, Fraternity, Equality' and bring about a similar revolution. It seems incredible that the quiet rural village of Morley should have produced a revolutionary but Robert Wilmot records in 1793 ...

> 'By the exertions of the disaffected this part of the Kingdom is brought into a state of nearly bordering on rebellion, but the prudent measures taken by men of better minds, will it is hoped put a stop to the growing spirit of Republicanism - or rather Disorder. In my own parish I know but one man (whose name is Alsop*) that has shewn the least wish to overturn the present system of government - that man has

endeavoured to instill into the minds of those with whom he is connected, principles of the most diabolical tendency, such as a total insubordination of all ranks and orders of men, and ideas of the justice of a perfect equality of property - hitherto his influence has had little effect, and I trust it will shortly be properly understood by those he would mislead'. He then continues 'Exclusive of this kind of political commotion my Parish is in a state of tranquility'.

*Alsop has a descendant still living in Morley who has a copy of a will made by Alsop's mother-in-law which ensures that none of the money she left would get into Alsop's hands.

Religion

Robert Wilmot made long comments each year and they deal with a variety of subjects. In 1788 he noted the King's illness ...

'King George III was seized with insanity and rendered incapable of transacting business... the secrecy which was observed about the court prevented its becoming public till necessity compelled the Ministers to make it known'. And in the following year he welcomed the increasing tolerance in religion that made it possible for Roman Catholic countries to celebrate the King's recovery with the Te Deum. 'A circumstance that must surely be looked upon as a happy presage of the downfall of Bigotry and Superstition, and the establishment of a pure system of Religion throughout Europe'. Perhaps it was just this hope for unity that made him so bitter against the Baptists who built a chapel in Smalley... 'With the exception of a few they have always been considered by me as the most worthless characters in my parish, and as I have never yet witnessed a change in their conduct to have been attendant on the change of their religious profession, I own I cannot divest myself of the opinion that their schism has more hypocrisy than religious zeal for its basis'.

SMALLPOX

Smallpox was endemic in England until well into the nineteenth century and there were always a number of deaths from this cause. While Robert Wilmot was Rector there was only one outbreak in Morley in 1779, and when we realise how little was known of the cause of the disease what he had to say was sound common sense...

'In the last year the smallpox went almost throughout the parish. In Morley thirty persons had it but only two died. In Smalley forty-three persons had it; twelve died that were buried there and a great number of children of the Methodists who had never been baptised were taken to Hallam to be buried.' (There was a burial ground for Non-Conformists at Kirk Hallam). 'In Morley they were kept clean which I suppose was the reason that so few died. In Smalley the case was different, a proof that cleanliness is the best preservative in this distemper'.

REJOICINGS

In 1788 Robert Wilmot records ...

'the 5th November being the 100th anniversary of the Revolution it was celebrated throughout the Kingdom, and I believe there was scarcely a village which did not show tokens of rejoicing upon the occasion except the village of Morley'.

Unfortunately no reason is given for this state of affairs.

It may however be connected with an event that occurred at the beginning of the century when George Sacheverell was High Sheriff and invited the celebrated Dr. Henry Sacheverell, a kinsman and Rector of St. Andrew's Holborn, to be his Chaplain.

According to custom the Sheriff's Chaplain preached the Assize Sermon in All Saints before the King's Judge and the Mayor, and in it he attacked the 'glorious revolution', denounced dissenters and preached passive obedience to kings. This sermon caused throughout England an uproar which rose to a real storm when the doctor repeated the sermon before the Lord Mayor of London in St. Paul's.

There is some doubt as to whether Dr. Henry Sacheverell was related to the Derbyshire family but it is said he was desirous of being thought a relation, and it appears some of the family were proud of the connection.

By 1801 however a more festive spirit prevailed... 'In the course of the year 1801 all the allies of Great Britain had withdrawn themselves from the war and submitted to the control of Republican France - the nation however was not dismayed by being left alone to the contests - on the contrary the National spirit seemed to rise as the difficulties and dangers increased... Upon the preliminaries being signed a general rejoicing took place, and cattle or sheep were roasted whole in almost every Township - in this Township two sheep were roasted, the one of them on the same wooden spit on which a sheep was roasted in the year 1760 on the conclusion of the German war'.

Robert Wilmot comes out clearly in his own writings as a just and sensitive man, deeply concerned for the people in his care, and loved and respected by them in return. He suffered increasingly from gout towards the latter part of his life, and some of his notes are written in an unfamiliar but still quite legible left hand. He died in 1803 at the age of fifty-three and it is recorded that his funeral 'shewed an assembly of the whole parish with tears and sadness on every face'.

Among the documents in the parish chest are some lines 'occasioned by a walk near Morley church in the summer of 1812' written by Tho. Boden and an extract reads:-

'...And when releas'd from school, oft have I strayed
   Down yonder path-way where the silver rill
   Mourns as it murmurs, near yon verdant shade;
And tells its sorrows to the neighbouring hill.

Mourns for its once loved Wilmot, now no more -
   His friendly hand, and cheering voice are fled;
   That voice that charm's the rich and cheer's the poor,
Lies buried now among the silent dead.

Yet some fair remnants of his taste remain
   As these sweet shades and spreading lawns can tell
   And fragrant groves encircling yonder fane
That echoes with the death-bell's solemn knell ...'

He is buried in the churchyard beneath the shade of an old horse chestnut tree to the right of the path leading to the vestry door with that of his wife Bridget who died in January 1829 aged seventy-nine - there is no record of any family. We record the epitaph before the inscription is obliterated by time.

If him thou knewst, good Friend who standest here
Pass gently on for he has laid thy fear,
But if in pensive ... thou art come
To muse upon the writing of the Tomb,
Here pause awhile and from an honoured name
Catch a pure spark to quicken in the flame.
For that which here returns to kindred ...
Is Wilmot once the friend the faithful knew,
The rich who loved him mourn him dead,
The poor will bless him for the Poor he fed.
Cheer'd by his smile the infirm would rejoice,
And age forgot its sorrow at his voice.
Oh! What a lesson then our Wilmot's name
Stranger farewell, depart and do the same.
If Rich be like him in a generous mind,
If Poor be like him for thou mayst be kind.
So when the last dread Trump shall rend the skies,
Then like him thou mays't hope in Joy to rise.

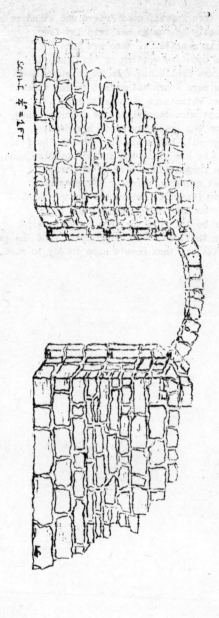

GATEWAY OF THE OLD MORLEY HALL, IN THE CHURCHYARD.

Scale ¾" = 1 ft

CHAPTER 8

MORLEY'S SCHOOLS

In 1816 a Church of England school was erected on Morley Moor; its exact position is unknown but it was in the vicinity of the almshouses. This school was set up by an endowment income of £11.0s.2d. from a charity founded by Emma Darwin in her will of 1818 giving £110.5s.0d. for this purpose. The school consisted of a schoolroom, 33 feet by 20 feet, and a statement in 1877 of the Trustees (R. Sitwell, R. Darwin and H. Bradshaw), gives the average attendance for six months as twenty-six scholars. Older members of the parish now recall their parents saying that when this school was in use the pupils had to pay a copper or so a week and take their own stools. The school was finally closed in 1879 and replaced later by a Board School which opened in the January of 1881. In the parish magazine for January 1910 there is a note 'that the old school house on the Moor has now been pulled down'. It is recalled that a house called Dames School used to stand by the side of the Moor Pond, but whether it was ever used as a school no-one can say for sure.

The new school was built on Main Road, and consisted of one large classroom which the children aged eight to thirteen years used. It had two cloakrooms and was staffed by a headteacher and two assistants. The school has not changed much although it seems to have undergone some rebuilding in 1897 when the infants room was added, and in 1911 when the Recreation Room was used as a temporary schoolroom before they moved into the 'new building'. Heating apparatus was also installed in 1911 and since then the school has been improved by the addition of piped water electricity and flush toilets. One of the cloak rooms has been turned into a kitchen for the dishing-up of the mid-day meals, (started in 1941) which are delivered ready cooked from a central kitchen.

The school log book for the years 1881 to 1907 has not been traced so little is known about this period, but the next log book from which the County Education Office have given permission for extracts of an historical nature to be used, gives us much interesting information.

Epidemics

Epidemics hit schools even today but the records of illnesses in the log book suggest how much more serious these were in the days before immunisation was common. Whooping cough, measles, diptheria, scarlet fever as well as ring-worm and skin infections are all mentioned. Curiously polio does not seem to have occurred. Today only measles is likely to cause a serious drop in attendance figures, and in 1928 during a measles epidemic the numbers in schools fell from a possible forty to only eight pupils. In 1918 the school was actually closed on medical grounds although we do not know for what illness but it may have been 'flu which can still spread with alarming rapidity. Diptheria and scarlet fever are almost unknown now among children. Apart from these epidemics school attendance seems to have been good for there are mention of half-holidays given in recognition of this.

The Welfare State and the increasing medical care of children show very clearly in the log book. After 1911 there was a regular medical inspection and in 1917 comes the first mention of a school dentist when children go to Derby for treatment by him. They were sent to the Clinic there too and sometimes were recommended for the Children's Hospital.

Weather

Bad weather affected Morley more than most schools. In 1912 sixty-one out of the eighty-one children on the register had more than a mile to walk to school,, and over field paths or unmade roads this was impossible in heavy snow. School work seems to have been disrupted nearly every January or February between 1910 and 1920.

Education Policy

Some entries show the changes that were taking place nationally. In 1913 when the school leaving age was thirteen, two children left immediately after their birthdays, but later children obviously stayed as they do now to the end of term when they reached the statutory leaving age. Despite the 1918 Act raising the leaving age to fourteen except for children going into jobs urgently, in 1921 a boy left at thirteen on a 'labour certificate'. Scholarship exams for the grammar schools are mentioned. The school nurse and a P.E. instructress visit the school, not only on their duties but also to give lessons. In 1928 the Hadow Report made recommendations about the methods of teaching and although no reference is made in the Morley log book, it might well have been that Morley in some ways was actually in advance of these ideas. Derbyshire must have been a fairly active county in education for the staff of the school were sometimes absent attending conferences or lectures. Certainly His Majesty's Inspectors visited the school regularly and encouraged new ideas in teaching. The idea of teaching being a trade however died hard, and as late as 1925 there is mentioned a teacher 'completing her period of apprenticeship'.

The Curriculum

The curriculum changes with the passage of years, and of course with the individual interests of the various headmistresses. The scope of subjects however is very impressive, and Morley must have had some progressive teachers. Schools today may have a wider range and the subjects may be more consistently taught, but there must be many pupils at school today who would envy Morley children of that time for the variety of lessons they enjoyed, yet this was done on very little money (the allowance for the year 1913 was:- fifty children at 3s.9d., three at 2s.9d., and nineteen infants at 2s.3d. so the total was only £17.18s.6d. from which all materials had to be bought).

In 1914 comes the first mention of Home Management; an H.M.I. report remarks 'original writing is encouraged by letting the children describe a picture postcard or other object brought from home, or subjects which demand observation, personal experience or imagination'; the School Nurse teaches the girls how to bath a baby and the P.E. instructress after taking the seniors for drill enquires if they have learned any dance steps. The children went to Derby for swimming lessons in 1920 and the girls went to Horsley Woodhouse to learn cookery. Particularly interesting is an extract of 1919 of how 'the children went to the field opposite the school to make a 'Village of Ancient Britain' with models they had previously made in the modelling lesson'. The school went to Breadsall and invited children from West Hallam for football and cricket matches, and outings to Derby to plays and films were made. In the 1930s visits to a blacksmith, a brickyard and the church were made and the introduction of geography walks strikes a very modern note. Indeed Morley records could well grace a present day Speech Day report.

The 1914-18 War

The record of the school during the 1914-18 war shows how much the war affected the lives of everyone. At first it was Miss Boden bringing Red Cross materials so that the children might make face flannels, and asking them to knit mufflers, caps and mittens. Later the Rector Mr. Bedford presented the school with a certificate for the work done. They had completed 95 mufflers, 26 caps, 6 pairs of mittens, 135 face cloths, 49 treasure bags and 14 pairs of socks.

Seven wounded soldiers from the Hospital set up in Morley at the Manor were no doubt exciting visitors in 1915, but Mrs. Lynn one of the teachers must have felt otherwise, for in 1916 she was granted leave of absence to visit her husband posted home wounded.

By 1918 the position of England had grown more desperate and the school was closed in February 'to enable the teachers to do visiting in connection with the Food Distribution Scheme' and again in the following month the school closed while the teachers helped with the scheme for Meat Rationing. The children were thanked for collecting wool from the hedges for the salvaging department, and an H.M.I., Mr. Vickers, visited the school 'to make enquiries about the collection of blackberries, and as a result 128 lbs. were sent off to the jam factory in Derby. There is ample suggestion here of how effective was the U-boat campaign and to what extent England was thrown back on her own resources.

<u>General</u>

Over this period the number on the register drops from eighty to forty, reflecting the trend for smaller families, but perhaps due more to the drift from the land. There were many teachers who came and went, ten head-teachers and twelve infant teachers from 1911 to 1929, but after 1921 the coming of Miss E. Woodford marked a more stable regime.

The school has on the whole been of a progressive nature, and the curriculum for a small village school has been varied and interesting from a practical as well as an academic point.

In 1977 there are 32 children on the roll.

CHAPTER 9
MORLEY MOOR CHAPEL

The deeds for the release of land for the first Chapel on Morley Moor are dated 1845 and the Chapel Registration Certificate, 1854. The building of the Chapel was carried out by Mr. Herbert Hollingsworth but it was converted into a dwellinghouse and the deeds transferred to James Ault and Miss Emily Ault in September 1892.

The deeds of the present Chapel were held by a Mr. John Wright and a Certificate of Registration for the new Chapel issued in 1861. The building is of stone and measures approximately 33 feet by 23 feet and a small kitchen and lavatory were added in the 1950s. With the installation of electricity in 1954, modern fan heaters replaced the old iron stove which for many years had warmed the place. It used to stand on the left-hand side as one entered the building between the congregation and the pulpit. The Chapel was connected up with the main drainage system in 1965.

Anniversary Sunday was celebrated for many years on Easter Day and was followed on the Monday by a tea in the Chapel with a short service, but this practice ceased four years ago. However when the Chapel had a thriving Sunday School the children sang and recited poetry and Methodists for miles around supported these Anniversaries.

Each year on the Monday evening following the Harvest Festival Sunday, the fruits and vegetables are sold by auction, the sale taking place in the Chapel and the proceeds going towards the upkeep.

The Elderly People's Association hold their monthly meetings and various other activities in the Chapel and services are now only held fortnightly on Sunday evenings.

CHAPTER 10

WITHIN LIVING MEMORY

We get glimpses of nineteenth century Morley from the Reverend Charles Kerry, author of two books on Smalley (which with Kiddesley Park was a chapelry of Morley until 1877). He also made copies of the Morley and Smalley Church Registers which are in the Derby Borough Library and to which he adds his own comments.

Morley Wakes were at one time a very grand affair and were held on September 21st, feast of St. Matthew, patron saint of the Church, and the Reverend Mr. Kerry describes them thus:-

Morley Wakes

'About the commencement of the nineteenth century when asses were much used for pack-saddle purposes, a yearly show of these animals was held during the Wakes Week at Morley Smithy, when many of them changed hands, and races were instituted to exhibit their quality. The competition was open to the neighbourhood and great was the rural excitement.

Mine host of the 'Three Horse Shoes' provided a cup for the winner, and Mr. Paul Fisher of Brackley Gate was steward and master of the course. Paul was a great man on these occasions. Attired in 'cock-and-pinch' hat, long waistcoat, knee boots and short breasted coat, riding whip in hand, his presence was felt everywhere. It was 'Mr. Fisher' from every quarter, though plain Paul on all other occasions. He was a great wag, full of humour, a genial companion, and half the life of the countryside.

Handbills of the races were printed, headed with an appropriate woodcut of grandstand, winning post, scales for weighing the jockeys etc. One of these printed in 1817 is now in the possession of Sir Henry H. Bemrose. Paul's donkey was named 'Ling Cropper' from its pasturage on the moor. Tailor Wheatcroft's steed was 'Prick-stitch' by 'Cabbage' and so on of the rest.

On one of these occasions a Smalley youth was seen struggling with his ass in a deep dyke by the roadside, into which the animal had conveyed his rider instead of securing the honours of the race, and despite all urging and coaxing, the creature would not move. "Hello, my lad" said the squire, who happened to be passing at the time

"When do the races begin?". "We are running now sir" was the jockey's response.

It was great sport on these occasions for the Morley youths to thwart or impede any outside competitors; a favourite trick being to push both steed and rider into some dyke or pond; and no doubt the Smalley candidate had been favoured with their attentions.'

By the beginning of this century however the donkey races had ceased, although there was still a gathering of the clans on Wakes Day. It is recalled that the 'Oddfellows Club' band setting off from the Rose and Crown 'played' their way down to the Three Horse Shoes where everyone waited impatiently for the Wakes to begin. Everyone joined in the fun and games, and the children ran races or made themselves dizzy on the roundabouts. The menfolk met for a reunion at the 'Smithy', where they challenged each other at skittles and feasted on beer and bread and cheese. During the celebrations one or two of the local 'big-nobs' would look in and pay for the jug to be filled up and passed round. Alas! the outbreak of the war in 1914 brought all such festivities to an end, and the Morley Wakes have never been revived.

Cheavening

An interesting job that was done by women to make a little extra money was cheavening. Mrs. Whiteman who died in 1943 at the age of ninety did this, and we had a record of her work from a member of the group.

Mrs. Whiteman lived in one of the almshouses in her later years and received work from Ilkeston, Woodhouse and Belper firms. She had learnt how to do it at the age of nine when her mother had pinned a sock to her arm to get the tightness that was essential for the work. A special fine round eye needle was used and in the early days the design was always of white silk, but later coloured silks were introduced to give a better effect. The designs of daisies

Morley Council School — Infant Class 1913

Mr. S.C. Slack, who still lives at Morley, and his father ploughing in 1943

The Mound

Ferriby Cottage, built 1857.

or bells or such patterns were worked at the ankle and up the leg. For some stockings only sixpence a dozen was paid, even though these were quite good stockings, but others would fetch a shilling a dozen pairs, depending on how neatly they were worked and on the intricacy of the design. One tree design or 'point' took perhaps a week or more to do and for this three shillings was paid, but this was a very special job. All the work had to be done very neatly, no knots were allowed and each length of thread was sewn back in. Sometimes Mrs. Whiteman would have to sit up all night to finish a consignment if the next lot of work was due the following day. On an average she earned seven shillings a week for this work.

Obviously working at night by artificial light was difficult on such fine patterns. This was overcome by filling a 3 lb. jam jar with water and placing it on a pile of books near the paraffin lamp. The flame was in this way reflected and threw more light on her work, and the jar moreover made a good magnifying glass.

Although this is one of the few skilled jobs that could be done by women in their homes that have lasted into this century, there must have been many women in Morley who helped in some such way to increase the family income.

The Stone Quarry, Morley Moor

The stone is described in Glover's History of Derbyshire as salmon coloured grit. Some of the best scythe stones were made here, also grindstones varying in diameter from eighteen inches to four feet and which sold at about forty shillings per ton, and about twelve hands were usually employed.

How these grindstones were made had been described by Mr. F. Wain who worked there as a young boy. 'After the top soil was cleared, a search would be made for any faults that appeared on the surface of the rock. Each man had eight wedges and a hammer and he would lightly tap the fault in the rock with the wedge until a crack was made, and it was then carefully levered out and down over the edge. The boys of the village would work by candlelight, first dipping the stones into a trough of water and than rubbing them against a rough stone in order to make them smooth. When the four sides were smooth, they were put into stacks called 'castles' and they usually completed about three dozen in a week. They were paid a penny for each stone completed.

Mr. F.S. Ogden remembers seeing the stone dressed. The dressing tool or 'pick' was a heavy iron head about nine or ten inches long with an approximate two inch square section slightly tapered. On one end was welded a projection rather like a bird's beak. The dresser worked standing astride the stone. He also saw evidence of a seam of coal in the extreme bottom towards the west.

The quarry closed down about 1917 and a house 'The Potlocks' was built on the site by Mr. R. Needham. The chains used at the quarry were laid in the foundations and the props, made of pitch-pine, were used in the timbers of the roof.

Ferriby Brook

A George 'Ferrebie' is mentioned in the Parish Registers in 1622 but whether this name is in any way connected with Ferriby Brook and House we have not been able to verify. The first mention of Ferreby Brook House is in 1767.

The present house stands on the main road near to the brook on the Morley/Breadsall boundary and has a date on it of 1857. One of the Derbyshire Journals of that year states that there was a beerhouse at Ferriby, and in 1891 a market gardener, florist and nursery man resided here.

One of Morley's Church Wardens, (c.1856), Mr. Joseph Whittaker F.R.G.S. a widely travelled man and a distinguished botanist, started a school here for boys. About twelve scholars attended usually after leaving school on the Moor at the age of eleven. There is a lecturn to his memory in the church dated 2nd March 1894.

A Mr. Larcombe lived here for many years until his death in 1947. He was a collector and an authority on antique china, and many were the distinguished visitors who came to Ferriby to view his collection.

* * * * * * * *

For a picture of the village in the latter part of the nineteenth century we are indebted to the memories of those, who Morley 'born and bred' were willing to recall for us scenes and tales of their youth.

The Postman

Mrs. Eliza Day who died at the age of 92 in 1969 vividly remembered the postman, Mr. James Hall, who, in the 1880s walked from Derby with the local mail. This journey took him along the Breadsall road past the Priory, up to Brackley Gate, then on down Cloves Hill to the Rose and Crown where he stayed until his return journey about 4.30 p.m. He took a slightly different route back. Leaving the Rose and Crown he passed Morley Manor, the Three Horse Shoes and Morley Bridge, where he cut off past the Mound and Tootle Pond along the lane to Mason Field, where he would give a loud blast on his whistle to announce his arrival at the far end of Breadsall Moor.

Mrs. Day remembered being sent to buy stamps from the postman as he passed down the Moor, and recalled how one had to pay for them, stick them on the letters and hand the letters back for posting. All this time she had to run along beside him to keep up with his big strides - the postman himself refusing to stop for anything or anyone. Anyone who wanted anything therefore made a point of being at the top end of the Moor to meet him when they heard his whistle blow in Mason Field.

The first record of a Post Office is in Kelly's Directory in 1891, and this gives a Mr. Charles Chapman as receiver. In 1895 he is listed as 'sub-postmaster, blacksmith and wheelwright, letters through Derby arriving at 8 a.m. and dispatched at 6 p.m., Postal Orders were issued but not paid.' Mr. Chapman lived in one of the cottages on Morley Bridge.

Mrs. Swindell of Church Farm became postmistress in 1900 followed by her grand-daughter Mrs. A. Parkinson. The present postmistress is Mrs. M. Marshall of Brick Kiln Lane, Morley who was appointed on 1st January 1972.

* * * * * * * *

Mr. H. Hunt who died this year at the age of 92 came of an old Morley family and many were the stories he recalled of events and everyday happenings in the village towards the end of the last century.

He remembered how his grandfather regularly used the old footpath to Stanley over the bridge. It was a good paved footpath and would easily take a horse and cart, and many journeys were made taking grain by pack-saddle to the windmill at Dale for grinding.

A fine avenue of oak trees grew alongside the path, and when felled towards the end of the 1914-18 war they were reported to be at least three hundred years old.

* * * * * * *

Mr. F.S. Ogden whose home was at Stanley wrote the following account of some of his earliest memories connected with Morley Church and Church Lane:

Church Lane and Bridle Road to Stanley

My parents 'settled' at Morley Church when I was a very small boy. The way to the Church from Stanley was over the railway bridge at 'Klondike'. 'Klondike' did not then exist as there was only the old cottage at the foot of the bridge approach.

'Skevington's Houses' were the first to be built by the owners of the land of that name. The bridle road was then well-used, also as a footpath and occasionally by vehicles. At the foot of the bridge approach on the Morley side were a hunting gate and a vehicle gate, the latter kept locked, which belonged to the Railway Company and were kept well painted white. There was a good stone paved ford across the brook as well as a footbridge. The down-stream edge of the paved ford was two or three feet above the level of the stream below so there was usually quite a waterfall except in a dry summer. I have seen trout in the stream below.

The house at the bottom of 'Potter's Lane' came to be known later as 'the Burnt House' because it was eventually burned down and remained derelict. It was then occupied by the Martin family. There was Mrs. Martin senior, a tall somewhat gaunt old lady, her son and his wife and a niece (Miss Palfree). All regularly attended Church and the old lady and the niece were in the choir. Below the 'Burnt House' alongside the footpath was a well-stocked apple orchard and behind that a large damson orchard. There was a deep well close to the gate into the land with the usual stone head and waller (the wooden roller and handle for lowering and raising the bucket).

The house at the top of the land opposite Moses Lane was occupied by an elderly couple. On particularly hot Sundays the old gentleman used to walk up Church Lane in his shirt sleeves (white starched) as far as the Rectory wall and then don his coat.

It was at first too far for me to walk all the way to church, so the first part of the journey was made in a two-wheeled vehicle of some prestige called 'The Peerless Car'. It was built to last and is still in going order! It used to be put in Mr. Hinds' joiners shop at the bottom of the land and from there the journey was completed on foot.

My mother remembered the Reverend H.H. Bradshaw[20] as Rector and was[21] present in Church when the Reverend C.J. Boden 'read himself in'. Consequently she knew the six consecutive Rectors each of whose names began with the letter 'B'.

Sheepwash

On the opposite side of the land from the joiner's cottage and a little higher up there was the sheepwash. A hand gate on the roadside led into a walled enclosure in which was the sunk 'wash' lined and paved with stone. The wash was fed from the ditch bringing the water from a spring in 'Donkey Hollow', from the cattle trough and the overflow of the Fishponds. The ditch was stopped and the water turned into the wash when required.

The Portway

An alternative return route for us was to turn off the lane through a stile almost opposite Moses Lane and go along the footpath on the line of the old Portway over the railway, and by footpath over the brook and eventually out into the lane near home. This however was only an occasional variation and strictly for dry weather. The first part of the Portway was between hedges and although a 'grass road' was hard underneath. It was said to have been used a good deal during the construction of the railway.

There were a number of old oak trees in the hedges and I have a water-colour of the largest, a very fine tree, which proved to be about 280 to 300 years old. Most of them were cut down when the Derby Co-op bought the Jesse Farm.

In those days there was quite a procession up Church Lane to morning service on Sundays. Four or five Martins from the bottom house; the top cottage; Deppers; Hunts; Hinds; Boswell and about five Skevingtons from Jesse Farm.

Another family the Whittaker's were staunch 'Victorians' and Mrs. Whittaker wore the victorian shawl on most occasions. It is on record that twice a year at any rate one could be sure of the date and that was when Mrs. Whittaker changed from summer shawl to winter shawl and vice versa, regardless of the weather.

A regular member of the congregation who used to sit in a seat behind the door (where the font is now) was an old man rather deformed and very lame who got about with difficulty on crutches. I think he used to go down to the Rectory every Sunday after service for a meal. He was known to us for identification as 'the old cripple'. At that time we had a young house boy who was fond of using any unusual and impressive words which he got hold of without regard to fitness. He also sat in a seat behind the door and one Sunday he returned from Church and announced that the 'old hypocrite' was not there.

Organ

The organ was blown by hand. A 'tell-tale' on the organ indicated when the wind was running out and also when the bellows or rather the 'wind box' was full - the latter condition also being announced by a 'mighty rushing wind' heard above the music. In the case of one blower whose attention used to wander a bit from the 'tell-tale' the first condition was not infrequent, and the organ would wail into silence and then burst out into a ff. of sound quite likely well behind the choir.

Peafowl

Peafowl were kept at the Rectory and were occasional and rather unwelcome visitors on the thatched roofs of stacks and also of a portion of Martin's house. During summer the church door was usually open during service and it was no uncommon thing to hear the Rector's voice answered from the porch or nearby by the rather piercing reply from a peacock. I remember one morning when only a quick sortie by someone near the door prevented some young pigs joining the congregation.

The Mausoleum

The building of the Sacheverell-Bateman mausoleum created a great deal of interest. The exhumation from the vault in the churchyard and installation of the coffin in the new building possibly created still more interest, certainly according to gossip, to one inhabitant, Mr. Bickerstaff. He was somewhat of a character apparently and determined to see what transpired. He is said to have climbed into one of the trees which it is not stated, and from that point of vantage to have kept an eye on the proceedings, but there does not seem to be any record of what he saw!

Beating the Bounds

One of the annual ceremonies was the walking of the boundaries which took place in most parishes to ensure that the boundaries were exactly known and that no parish infringed on another's land. A few of the older Morley families recall that the party 'beating the bounds' set off armed with spades, and at various points of the boundary a hole would be dug and one of the young lads seized and stood in the hole head first. This was to impress upon him the exact boundary so that he would always remember it and he was given a halfpenny or a penny piece as a consolation. The last time this took place was around 1870.

Harvest Supper

One of the great occasions of the year were the Harvest Suppers given by the farmers for their workers and Mr. Hunt remembered his father talking about those that were held in the stable yard at the Hall by invitation of Mr. R. Sitwell after the harvest had been gathered in.

The menu consisted of good roast beef, bread potatoes and home-brewed beer, and the entertainment was provided by Mr. Jospeh Moss of Smalley, a violinist of some ability and a notable singer. One of his songs was 'The Beggars Ramble' - this included in its verses a mention of all the surrounding villages and inns, and the 'Smithy' and beerhouse at Ferriby Brook are duly mentioned. Mr. Hunt had a copy of this song which belonged to his father.

The Annual Flower Show

The Flower Show was organised by the Rector, Mr. Boden, and the last one took place in 1914. Local competition was strong and entries came in too from surrounding villages. There was a display of hothouse plants from the 'big-houses' - Broomfield, the Manor and the Priory, and the Rector gave a prize for the best kept cottage garden.

The Rectory grounds were filled with swingboats and coconut shies, and entertainers and acrobats from Derby added to the fun, whilst the village children showed their skill in dancing round the maypole.

A band from Dale Abbey came on foot up Church Lane to play during the afternoon. They returned in the evening full of goodwill after the lavish refreshments, and played all the way down the lane to the great delight of the children who marched with them - a favourite tune being "The girl I left behind me" !

Queen Victoria's Diamond Jubilee

The Diamond Jubilee celebration was recalled by Mr. Hunt. It was a day of great excitement with a tea-party in the Park followed by games and children's races. A brass band (probably from Dale) played throughout the afternoon and everyone was presented with a special Diamond Jubilee mug. Each child was given a newly minted sixpence - a gift to each child in the Ilkeston constituency by Mr. T.H. Hooley (philanthropist) who was putting up for parliament at the time. Mr. Hunt treasured his sixpence all his life.

A fountain with drinking cup and chain together with a horse trough were erected at the junction of Church Lane. These were the gifts of the Rector, Mr. C. Boden, and his sister in honour of the occasion.

Choirboys' Outing

Mr. Hunt also remembered how the usual outing was a day trip to Skegness by train. All this sounds quite modern but in 1897 and probably because of the Diamond Jubilee celebrations the trip was a local one to Matlock. Two horse-drawn wagonettes filled with choirboys set off from Morley, going round by Breadsall to avoid the steep hill at Little Eaton. Such a trip is hard to imagine today, but they went on to do what a similar party today would do - climbing about on the rocks and then going to tea in one of the hotels. After the tea a marble clock was presented to the organist, Mr. Arnold, for his twenty-five years of service at Morley.

King Edward VII's Coronation

This was recalled by a member of the group who was a child at the time and it followed much the same pattern as the Jubilee. The King himself was dangerously ill but the national festivities went on although the Coronation itself had to be postponed. The most memorable moment of the day was when the Rector announced that news had come through that the King was out of danger.

* * * * * * * *

Mr. Hunt himself was lucky to survive for he recalled a tale told him many times by his mother:

In a small low-roofed cottage in Church Lane (now derelict) lived the parish clerk Mr.Boswell and his family.

After the wedding of his school-teacher daughter to a local stonemason named Slater, all the relatives, friends and neighbours crowded into the tiny cottage for the reception including Mrs. Hunt with young Henry in her arms.

This was too good an opportunity to be missed for a local practical joker named Beardsley, for after wedging the door of the cottage so that it couldn't be opened, he climbed up the sloping roof and hastily began to block up the chimney with grass clods.

As can be imagined the room very quickly filled with smoke, and as it was sometime before the door could be forced open, several guests were overcome by fumes and collapsed, and great anxiety was felt for Mrs. Hunt's young baby. However he duly recovered and continued to thrive!

Memories of Morley School (recalled by Mrs. Day and Mr. Hunt)

In the latter part of the last century the headmistress was Miss Taylor with Miss Lakin as her assistant. Miss Taylor had a schoolmaster brother at Breadsall, but she lived with her mother at the School House at Morley.

Mrs. Esther Taylor is remembered as a very

kind old lady and the children were very fond of her. Each year on her birthday she baked a good big batch of gingerbread and gave all the children a neatly wrapped packet to take home with them for tea.

Mrs. Esther Taylor knew the children well for she taught many of them at Sunday School which was held in the schoolroom on Sunday mornings. The Rector, the Reverend Charles Boden, taught the older children, many of whom had left school and were now working, but they still enjoyed their Sunday school. They would practice the hymns to the playing of the Harmonium before walking in pairs over the Park to Church, the Reverend Mr. Boden leading the way.

Several Sunday School parties are remembered. Some at the Priory and others at Broomfield Hall by invitation of Mr.and Mrs. Schwind. There would be sports and prize-giving and the excitement of trying to keep perfectly still while a photograph was taken. Some of the old photographs have survived and show the boys neat and tidy and the girls fresh and shining with their hair done up in ribbons. Afterwards they would go inside the big house for tea. The wonderful scent of the roses in the glasshouses is something Mr.Hunt looked back on with nostalgia.

Mrs. Eliza Day had a sampler she made at school in 1891 at the age of fifteen, having been allowed to stay on to make up for time lost whilst in hospital. On numerous occasions she received the yearly prize of half a sovereign for needlework (given by the Rector Mr. Boden).

<u>The Reverend Charles Boden</u>

The Reverend Charles Boden was Rector of Morley from 1883 until his death in 1917. He never married but lived with his sister at the Rectory both sharing a keen interest in gardening. Not only his own garden but the adjoining churchyard were delightful with their personal oversight and work. He was a real lover of nature and many will recall him standing on the lawn with the white fantails circling round, while at his feet would be two or three stately peacocks.

The peacocks were a great fascination for the village children who loved to listen to their squawk as they strutted the turf, and now and then displayed their beautiful fans, and they would sit on the seat under the old tree at 'shedding time' eagerly watching for any of the tail feathers to fall. These would be carefully hoarded and brought out and admired for many a week after.

He was one 'given to hospitality' and many and various were the parties privileged to be entertained at the Rectory. 'Quiet Days' and conferences for clergy were frequently held here also Mother's Meetings, Boy Scouts and Girls' Friendly Societies from other parishes held their outings here and spent peaceful afternoons in the lovely gardens, so gay in the springtime with daffodils and fragrant in the summer with roses. Tradition has it that the first rambler type roses in the district were those planted by Mr. Boden at Morley.

Many of the entertainments and club activities that thrived in Morley at the turn of the century were organised and supported by the Rector, and he was President of the Cricket Club and interested too in Morley's very successful football team. He was himself a keen sportsman and would find time for occasional runs with the Meynell.

During the winter he organised weekly entertainments at the Recreation Room - whist playing, concerts, magic lantern shows, musical evenings, and the like. One of the older villagers recalls with nostalgia the music of the Peak Banjo Mandolin and Guitar Band which frequently came from Derby. There was also a library for the young boys, when books such as Robinson Crusoe and 'tales of darkest Africa' kept them spellbound.

People from the neighbouring villages would also join in the activities, leaving their horses and traps at the nearby farms. The ladies would find something for their enjoyment in the Recreation Room and the menfolk would play cards in the stable-room below.

At Christmas time a ball was held and one or two of the local youths would dress up in borrowed swallow tails and top hats. The Rector always attended but usually sat by the stove busy with his knitting, keeping a watchful eye for any rough play, and many of the village youths would be reprimanded for 'spinning the ladies off their legs' in the Lancers or Quadrilles'.

His knitting would often be for the choirboys, for on Christmas morning after the service the boys would go to the Rectory where they were given a mince-pie, an orange, and a pair of gloves, socks or a scarf knitted by the Rector.

One local event that caused quite a stir in Morley was the burning of the church in the neighbouring village of Breadsall in June 1914. No-one was ever convicted for the outrage but suffragettes were blamed. People had been seen loitering near the churchyard although descriptions were very conflicting. The day before the burning two strange women were seen near Morley church and were kept under close observation by the Rector, Mr. Boden, and his staff until they were safely off the premises. After the Breadsall church fire the Rector hastily summoned a meeting and formed a band of volunteer watchmen to patrol and guard the church at Morley until the danger subsided. Mr. Allsop recalls that one night whilst they were patrolling a warning shot was heard. Everyone immediately hurried to the scene ready to detain the 'suffragettes' only to find a very red faced volunteer watchman, who arriving late for duty had in his haste stumbled over one of the trip wires and caused one of the guns to fire.

* * * * * * * *

The 1914 war brought many changes in the life of the village with many of its young men away, and everyone must have felt grateful to Mrs. Lister-Kaye for her part in bringing Morley so early into the war effort, for the Derbyshire Advertiser of October 1914 reports:-

> 'Mrs. Lister-Kaye has turned Morley Manor into a hospital and it is attached to one of the base hospitals in the Northern Command, being now full of wounded men from the recent battle of the Aisne. They arrived at Derby Midland Station on Monday and were cheered by a large crowd outside, whilst the whole of Morley village turned out to bid them welcome.'

A cross and roll of honour was erected in the churchyard and a memorial plaque in the Church and Recreation Room in honour of those who gave their lives in the Great War. An inscription reads:-

Leiut. H.A.C. Topham Indian Army Attd. Welsh Regt.
Leiut. Ronald Greenfield 1st Batt. The Rifle Brigade.
Capt. W.K.S. Haslam R.F.A.
Pte. Frederick T. Legge 5th Dorsetts.
Pte. George R. Clowes 4th Worcesters.
Gnr. John Allsop R.F.A.
Gnr. John Skevington R.G.A.
Pte. Charles Hunt Durham Lt. Infy.
Gnr. William Radford R.F.A.
Lce. Cpl. Frank Daws K.R.R.
Pte. Harry Pepper South Staffs.
Pte. William T. Clowes 3rd Sherwood Foresters
Pte. Percy Lowe Lancs. Fusiliers.
Emdr. William Hunt R.F.A.

1939-45
Gnr. C.R. Wasley - 1 - 16 - H.A. - R.A.
Sgt. V.P. Thompson W.O.P. A.G. - R.A.F.V.R.

War-time incident

During the 1939-45 war a lone German plane

flew across on a line roughly in the direction 'Three Horse Shoes' - Jesse Farm. No-one could imagine why the occupants should decide to drop bombs on that line but two were sent down. One was a 'firebomb' and the other a medium high-explosive of the 'whistling type'. The former which was of the 'petrol drum' kind landed in the middle of a field between the Jesse Farm and the railway. It made a sizeable dint in the ground and burnt out harmlessly. The other hit the railway embankment on the side towards the farm and scooped out a hole but without actually damaging the lines other than moving them slightly. The appearance and sound of the falling bombs quite belied the amount of damage.

* * * * * * * *

A 'Comforts' Fund was organised by the villagers during the last war for the men away in the forces. They were sent money at Christmas and also at Easter if funds allowed. The money was raised chiefly by whist drives held in the homes of supporters, and the accounts for 1940 show that twenty-four men were each sent ten shillings at Christmas.

Relics from the past

A late bronze age hollow-bladed riveted spearhead dating from 1200 - 1000 B.C. was in the early 1960s found on Morley Moor and was identified at Derby Museum where it is now on show. Several flint arrowheads, roman coins and fragments of early pottery were also uncovered in the area.

A number of stone figure-heads which have been in a garden of a house near to the Church for well over a hundred years were photographed and the prints studied by an expert who expressed an opinion that they were probably early sixteenth century although a personal inspection would be necessary before a definite opinion could be given.

　　How the figure-heads came to be in the garden and where they originally came from is open to conjecture. Whether they were from the Old Hall which was dismantled about the middle of the eighteenth century or whether they came from Dale Abbey with some of the treasures to the church it is not yet known. So they remain - interesting relics that have survived the years.

THE BUTTER CROSS

CHAPTER 11
THE REVEREND SAMUEL FOX M.A.

The Reverend Samuel Fox M.A. who was born on 11th February 1801 and died 7th September 1870 was the son of Edward Fox of Derby. He started his education at Derby School and his name and date of 1816 is one of hundreds to be found carved on the walls and panels of the old school building in St. Peter's Churchyard.

In October 1821 he proceeded to Pembroke College, Oxford, where apparently his career was not crowned with the kind of distinction that usually falls to the lot of studious and scholarly men - indeed there is no mention of him in any university class list. He left in 1825 and three years later became an M.A. having in the meantime prepared himself for ordination and probably taken Holy Orders. In 1829 he accepted the curacy at Morley and married in the 1830s, succeeding to the livings of Morley and Smalley in 1844.

He is described as one of the most learned Anglo-Saxon scholars of the day, and wrote many books on the subject, and his achievements led in due course to his election as a Fellow of the Society of Antiquaries, and secured for him the esteem and friendship of the pioneer of Anglo-Saxon study in England, Dr. J. Bosworth, (also a Derbyshire man) being born at Etwall and educated in the neighbouring village of Repton.

He had a lifelong interest in gypsies, although his published works apparently contain no hint of this, but he did not seriously continue his gypsy studies after about 1840.

Several years after his death two notebooks were discovered among his literary remains, containing Romani vocabularies set out side by side with Bryant's Glossary for 1785. These were preserved by his daughter Miss Anna Fox. The earlier notebook is entitled "A vocabulary of the Zingara or Gypsey Language" - the second and larger one bears the same title but has several additions, including a preface and a shorter list of Romani equivalents taken from 'Viney' Boswell at Smalley. The preface with which the larger of the two notebooks begins reveals that the Smalley vocabulary 'was commenced in consequence of an encampment being made near the village of Smalley in the winter of 1832-3. The writer of these remarks we are told, frequently visited them (the gypsies) and sat with them round their Everl(asting) fire - they were remarkably well conducted and three or four females and as many men attended divine worship at Smalley Chapel'. The name of the tribe was Boswell and the head of it, one Lawrence was looked upon as King of the Gypsies but the family themselves laughed at the idea, and asserted that no gypsy tribe lay claim to the distinction of Royalty. However the Derby Mercury records Lawrence Boswell's death and 'as proof that he was of some consequence among the fraternity, many tribes of gypsies from distant quarters assembled to bid him a last farewell'. The words recorded from Vaini (Viney) Boswell by Samuel Fox were obtained after the preface to the second notebook had been written and it is thought that the most likely date is 1839 for on April 7th of that year Samuel Fox baptised at Smalley, Cornelius, grandson of Vaini Boswell.

Miss Fox recalls that the Boswells used to camp in a lane near Morley in the late 1840s or early 1850s, and she was often taken by her father when a child to see them. There were two brothers, Moses and Aaron Boswell, but it was Moses and his family who came to Morley most frequently.

As a parish priest Samuel Fox was conscientious and thoroughly capable, whilst his kindness, graciousness and sensibility, and his occasional 'gleams of humour' must have made his tall, slightly stooping figure a welcome sight to most of his parishioners.

He rendered a lasting service to Morley by undertaking a much needed restoration of its ancient and interesting church, a work very near to his heart, for he was a close student of ecclesiastical architecture, though he never wrote on it save for his "History of Morley" which was published in 1872 two years after his death.

His obituary in the Derby Mercury states that 'his death was sudden, for he had previously been in full intellectual vigour. Only a few weeks earlier he had spent a short time at Oxford with his old friend, Professor Bosworth, examining the manuscript stores of the Bodlean Library for facts relating to the "History of Morley" which he had prepared for the press'.

He is buried at Morley and there is a bronze plaque to his memory in the church.

The above information has been gathered from various sources:-

The Derby School Register, The Derby Mercury and particularly "Samuel Fox and the Derbyshire Boswells" by T.W. Thompson, extracted from the Journals of the Gypsy Lore Society.

CHAPTER 12

THE VILLAGE TO-DAY

Morley is still a very rural village but changes have gradually taken place. Electricity was the first amenity to arrive in 1922 although the Church and the Three Horse Shoes were not connected until 1930. A small sub-station was erected next to the School on the Main Road. Piped water from the Derwent Valley has been available since 1936.

A bus shelter was erected in 1939 at Morley Bridge (paid for by money left over from the Coronation celebrations). The other four bus shelters in the parish were provided later by the County Council.

Street lighting and sewerage disposal are now complete services, Almshouses Lane and Morley Lane being the last to be connected to the main sewerage in August 1965.

The two old stone quarries on the Moor and Brackley Gate have been used by the local Council for tipping refuse, much to the annoyance of local inhabitants.

A Parish Council was formed in 1931 and meetings take place in the school at regular intervals. It is responsible for keeping the local authorities in touch on any matters requiring attention to roads, footpaths, housing, bus shelters, lighting etc.

Sixteen houses and four bungalows were erected by the County Council and completed early in 1962 in Brick Kiln Lane. The field used was at one time well-known for its primroses, so Primrose Drive was chosen as a name for the new area. The occupants are chiefly Morley people. More recently, several houses have been built in Brackley Gate and Cloves Hill. A number of old condemned cottages at the bottom of Almshouses Lane were demolished in 1966 and three houses and a bungalow erected on the site. The large cottage by the side of the Moor Pond has also been demolished and a house and bungalow erected immediately in front. The pond was also filled in. This land, which is one of the oldest parts of Morley, with its seventeenth century Sacheverel Almshouses, has since lost much of its charm. The Almshouses are in reasonable repair and are occupied by any elderly who qualify, single women and married couples, as well as men laid down in the original bequest.

There are still many varieties of wild flowers to be found although they are decreasing, and the Derbyshire Naturalists Trust acquired in 1966 its first nature reserve in the village in an effort to preserve the rare and other plants in the area.

A Women's Institute was formed in February 1950 with a membership of fifty-two. The first officers were:- President, Miss D. Topham; Secretary, Mrs. M. Slack; and Treasurer, Mrs. J. Morley. As Morley is a very scattered village the Women's Institute has played a great part in bringing its womenfolk together. Meetings are held monthly and are of an educational and social nature.

An association for the elderly people of the parish was formed in 1957 by Mr. and Mrs. M. Bladon with a committee comprising representatives from the various organisations in the village. Monthly meetings are held in the Chapel room in Almshouses Lane and a summer outing and Christmas party arranged each year.

Mr. and Mrs. M. Bladon were also responsible for starting a Youth Group in 1957, but this was taken over and organised as a Church Youth Group in 1962. This was disbanded during 1963 whilst extensive repairs were made to the Recreation Room. It was reformed in the autumn of 1964 by the County Youth Service who invited representatives from the various organisations in the village to form an Adult Management Committee, but eventually the Club was forced to close from lack of support.

There is a branch of the British Red Cross Society in the village. Miss M. Adams is the Township Leader and together with a committee has been actively engaged in raising funds and giving help wherever it is needed for many years.

Broomfield Hall

Broomfield Hall was purchased by the Derbyshire County Council in 1947 from Mrs. Crompton, the widow of the previous owner, who was very interested in the Hall becoming the new centre of agricultural education for Derbyshire, to be known then as the Farm Institute. Mr. J.R. Bond who had been Agricultural Education Officer for the County since 1914, became the first Principal. 425 acres (170 ha) of land were also purchased or tenanted, comprising Broomfield Farm, Lime Farm, Old Top Farm, Tunnel Farm, Church Farm and Brook Farm, to form the college farms for teaching and practising farm skills and demonstrating good farming.

The first thirty-six students were nearly all ex-servicemen. By 1953 there were forty men on the one-year residential course and many day-release students. In April 1954 Mr. P.A. Missen became Principal and in the same year a large hostel and Assembly Hall were opened. The first ten women students attended in 1955 taking the same course as the men.

Additions to the teaching facilities included a machinery workshop in 1957 and subsequently a new set of farm buildings to be called New Top Farm, comprising a piggery in 1957 and a new range of cattle buildings in 1959 with a milking parlour. New farm staff houses were added. The Old Top Farm at Morley Bridge was demolished. Eventually Church Farm tenancy was concluded and the County bought some land west of Lime Farm and north-east of Breadsall Cross Roads. In the sixties teaching workshops, lecture rooms, laboratory, demonstration ring and more farm buildings replacements increased the facilities to meet the educational needs of farming for Derbyshire.

The present Principal, E.V.J. Bathurst Esq. B.Sc., was appointed from 1st January 1976. At that time farm buildings and land were combined into the College Farm to be managed as one unit so as to provide optimum facilities for profitable farming, combined with the increased use of the farm for the teaching and practice.

Broomfield Hall now houses the female students, the dining and kitchen facilities and the administrative offices of the College. Many of the original fireplaces, ceilings and excellent wooden fittings are still preserved.

Finally, as time marches on, the Turret Clock above the old stables (now the Annexe) was made and installed by Smith of Derby in 1873. It is still in its original form - handwound, pendulum, non-striking; and is still keeping excellent time - a good example to those who observe it daily! It must tick on to measure the progress in farming and in gardening and to mark the careful preservation and continuance of all that is so good and pleasant and lasting in the country way of life;while those beneath it surge with the vitality and vigour of modern youth, tempered by mother nature into sons and daughters of the soil.The future well-being of Broomfield Hall and Estate will then be well assured.

Morley Rectory

In 1959, the Rectory became the Diocesan Retreat and Conference House. To this building, but detached from it, was added a twenty-four room dormitory block and the House and new block together accomodate a maximum of forty people.

Christian Societies from all parts of the country visit Morley, many of them returning year after year.

The Reverend R.P. Stacy Waddy was appointed Rector of Morley and first Warden of the Diocesan Retreat and Conference House in 1959 and was made an Honorary Canon of Derby Cathedral in October 1963. He was succeeded in 1967 by the Reverend G.W. Burningham,[23] who served as Rector until 1972.

In 1972, following the closure of the Retreat House (Red House) in the Southwell Diocese the Retreat and Conference House at Morley became a joint venture for the Dioceses of Derby and Southwell. Responsibility for domestic management of the House was then undertaken by Sisters of the Community of St. Lawrence at Belper who had performed similar duties at the Red House. The appointment of Rector of Morley has been in suspense since 1972.

This year the Sisters have returned to the Community and a new Warden and Housekeeper have been appointed.

Population

At the time of going to press, the population of the village is 439.

Most of the working population travel out of Morley each day to the many industrial and commercial enterprises in the neighbouring town of Derby and surrounding area. Teaching staff from many schools in the area live in the village. The numbers employed on the farms has decreased considerably due largely to farm mechanisation and economics. Trades in the village include a builder, plumber, welder and landscape gardener. There is one public house, but still no shop or garage.

CHAPTER 13

THE GEOGRAPHICAL BACKGROUND

Lying some 4 miles north-east of Derby, Morley is a small scattered village situated among the green uplands which divide the industrial tracts of the Middle Trent Valley from those of the great coalfield to the north. What it lacks in size however, it compensates for in its interesting diversity of geological formation and associated topography, for within its boundaries lies the junction of the carboniferous rocks of the Pennines with the triassic rocks of the Midland Plain. Many vague lines have been drawn in an attempt to delimit the boundary of the Midlands and North, but this geological boundary is probably the truest, so that in reality Morley stands as it were, with one foot in each region.

This section attempts to describe Morley's geographical character, so that if it is to be fully understood it should be used in conjunction with a good Ordnance Survey Map, and herein lies a problem since Morley lies at the line of intersection of several sheets. However, as regards the 1/50,000 map, "Derby and Burton-on-Trent", sheet 128 covers most of Morley and neighbourhood and has the advantage of showing the village in its regional setting, but a small eastern part lies on sheet 129 "Nottingham and Loughborough". For anyone with more than a passing interest, the most satisfactory map is the 1/25,000 sheet which possesses the double advantage of compactness and detail - the bulk of the village will be found on sheet S.K. 34 "Belper", but sheets S.K. 44, 43 and 33 are needed to show considerable tracts on the eastern and southern margins of the Parish.

We have dealt so far with the history of the village, and here we look at its past geography, or rather its distant prehistory as manifested in its rocks and soils, and this is no less fascinating than their diversity. For instance, the triassic plateau in the central area, with its rusty red soils and rocks (the colour being caused by iron oxide due to deposition in a dry climate) show that ions of time ago the Morley area must have been a red and arid desert. The coal measures on the other hand indicate formation in a subtropical climate, whilst the coming of the glaciers, as evidenced by the deposits of glacial drift, must have plunged the district into arctic conditions. With this in mind we can now take a more detailed look at Morley's varied topography.

It will be seen from the accompanying sketch map that the area takes the form of a plateau averaging some 400 - 500 feet above sea level, dropping steeply away to the west and north and more gradually to the south and east. Much of this plateau is composed of marls, sandstones and pebble beds, but the higher and more broken sections in the north-west lie over grits and shales, whilst the eastern slopes are developed over the Lower Coal Measures.

The Coal Measures form part of the great coalfield which extends north and eastwards into Yorkshire and Nottinghamshire, but within the Parish boundary is found the extreme south-western limit of these rocks, a boundary marked approximately by a line drawn from the summit of Cloves Hill in the north and extending via Littlewood and Morley Rectory to the top of Stanley Hill. East of this line lie the rocks of the Lower Coal Measures made up of a varying mixture of shales, coal seams and sandstones. These give rise to undulating country between 250 - 400 feet above sea level which slopes gradually down to the valley of the Stanley Brook, which has some fairly large tracts of Alluvium and some marsh - a fact indicated by its many attendant willows and alders. Several minor streams flow eastwards to join the brook, and these have low rounded interfluves rising some 50 - 100 feet above the valley floors. These north-south indentations combined with the general west-east slope of the country give rise to pleasant rolling, rounded hills. A well marked feature of the area is found in the sandstone outcrop, coincident with the prominence which extends from Morley Lane Stanley to the 400 feet contour north-west of Hayes Park Farm. This forms small, but quite steep bluffs where it approaches the Stanley Brook, especially on the eastern side.

In the north-eastern part of the Parish the country is markedly more open, having the appearance of a large amphitheatre centred on the valley of a small brook to the south-west of Hayes Wood. The appearance of this area however has been modified by opencast workings (there have been five sites in the Parish) since in this district there outcrops a seam of high quality Kilburn coal, which prior to these workings could actually be traced for one quarter of a mile northwards in the vicinity of Hayes Farm. Despite the effect of these opencast workings, the countryside here is not unpleasant since it backs on to the green slopes of Hayes Wood, and has the appearance of open park-like country. In Morley we are only concerned with the Lower Coal Measures, but it is interesting to note that in the extreme north-east of the Parish is found an outcrop of Silkstone or Clod Coal which marks the western limit of the much worked Middle Coal Measures.

Still forming part of the carboniferous series but giving rise to somewhat more rugged country are the grits and shales over which the north-western part of the Parish is developed. These in fact give rise to the most prominent feature of the district, in the heath-clad summit of Drum Hill which rises to a height of 514' above sea level. This hill and much of Breadsall Moor lies on Kinderscout Grit, an extremely rough gritstone which is evident in the stone walls which divide the fields in the area. In general the grits and shales give rise to a flat topped prominence falling steeply away some 350 - 400' to the valleys of the Derwent and Bottle Brook in the west, and northwards into the firs and birches of the combe-like Carr Brook Valley. Southwards the geology underlying the landscape is rather more complex, there being various shales which have been indented with the valleys of several small brooks and on the whole the slopes are less abrupt owing to a partial covering of Boulder Clay. The landscape here presents a picture of rounded hills, to which in parts the parklands of Breadsall Priory have contributed to give a very pleasant effect. Turning eastward an abrupt change of scenery occurs with the break of slope corresponding with the woodland fence to the east of Drum Hill (which is also the Parish boundary). This is in fact the junction of the massive Kinderscout grits with a more complex series of finer grits and shales, whose varying resistances to erosion have left their mark on the ups and downs of Moor Road. It was the finer grit of this group which was used to make the scythe and grindstones produced by Morley Quarry. Turning back to the Moor Road area, an interesting feature is to be found in the deposit of boulder clay which lies at the junction with Brick Kiln Lane in the vicinity of the old Brickyard. This clay was of course deposited by glaciers during the Ice Age and contains stone fragments, thought to have been carried by the ice from as far away as Yorkshire. In the north of the gritstone district, that is in the Brackley Gate area, is found a deposit of extremely rough grit, which gives rise to steep slopes falling rapidly northwards some 200 feet to the Lower Coal Measures and which affords some excellent views extending as far as Minninglow and Stanton Moor in the Peak District. The view from here, especially in clear weather after rain, is one never to be forgotten.

So far, the marginal tracts of the Parish only have been dealt with, so we must now turn to the heartland of Morley. That is the plateau on which the nucleus of the village is found, as has been noted this plateau is composed of red marls, sandstone and pebble beds which give rise to an almost flat plateau surface of some 425 - 450 feet above sea level. In the west, this plateau merges almost imperceptibly with the gritstone area, but the junction with the Coal Measures is quite well marked, especially in the south-eastern part of the Parish near the church where the sandstone, pebble beds and red keuper marls give rise to a small but bold front rising some 80 - 100 feet and overlooking the broad valley of the Stanley Brook. These formations have been deeply incised by two small streams, and the most northerly of these produces a rather wild brackeny little ravine known locally as the Gripps, in which the nature of the underlying rock is well evidenced. The more southerly stream has produced the sheltered hollow in which the village lies, and this, together with the fact that here the porous pebble beds abut on to the impermeable keuper to produce a spring line, was probably the dominant factor in the siting of the village. West and south of the church extend the red marl of the plateau which has lent a red tint to the soil so much in evidence along the line of the main A 608 road.

In various locations among the marls of the plateau, may be found further pebble beds such as those found to the east of Almshouses Lane in the vicinity of Broomfield Hall and south of the railway at the head of the Ferriby Brook. Generally these have little effect on the landscape except to produce gradual slopes southwards and save where old gravel pits have left minor humps and declivities. Turning southwards along the line of Lime Lane the plateau narrows to a neck between the valleys of the Stanley and Ferriby Brooks before broadening into Chaddesden Common. Here, in the south-east of the Parish, there is a much more continuous cover of boulder clay than elsewhere so that steep slopes are generally absent and the soils lack the red colouring of those further west, tending towards a dull buff.

Thus we have attempted to describe Morley's physical character, and though in 1500 years of human occupance the sequence of clearance, enclosing, emparking and extraction has substantially altered the superficial appearance of the landscape, the hills and the valleys remain much as they were. This then is the background to which Morley's history has been played - events not earth shattering, but nevertheless, events which form the fascinating story of a typical English village.

DIALECT WORDS HEARD IN MORLEY DURING THE LAST TEN YEARS

Whittle - to fret, to worry.
Twitchell - narrow lane between houses.
Twitch - couch grass (1595).
Slang - long narrow strip of land (1610).
Addle - (lit. cow urine? e.g. Addled egg.
Addle - (lit. to confuse) e.g addle pate - confused person.
Addle - (lit. property) to earn e.g. to addle one's keep (1580).
Wraps - (lit. coils or rings 1523) - entrails.
Kek, Kekay - hollow stemmed plant - cow parsley, dry stalk - as dry as a kek.
Soof, suff, sough - underground drain, used extensively in the reports of the Overseer of the Highway for Morley.
Fleake - an obsolete form of flake or hurdle, a temporary gate.
Tundish - funnel used formerly to fill the tun i.e. beer barrel.
Lap - to wrap.
Lap - to take up liquid with the tongue i.e. as a cat.
Fodderam - (lit. dry food for cattle) feeding passage for cattle.
Bing - (lit. heap or pile 1513) feeding place.
Drugget - coco matting.
Wintercracks - Bullaces, hedge fruit.
Frit - frightened.
Snap - (lit. slight or hasty meal 1631) cold packed food.
Boozen - manger.
Nesh - (lit. tender 1530) susceptible to cold.
Sile - (lit. strainer 1459) strainer of milk.
Sile - description of very heavy rain (1703) 'It siled down'.
Jitty - entry between houses.
Dab in - to work hard.
Mardy - spoilt.
Firk - to scratch or scrape like a hen.
Clemned - starved.
Frem - fresh - usually said of the lush Spring grass.
Moggy - a mouse (Derbyshire) elsewhere a cat!
Sprassin - courting.
Codged - rough job.
Clarty - thick, cloying, e.g. food thick on the tongue.
Maslin kettle - pan formerly used to cook maslin (a mixture of wheat rye and maize) now used for a preservative pan.
Cofer, coffer - Chest with a lid (often mentioned in eighteenth century Derbyshire farm inventories).
Cread - a milk pudding which has creamed by very slow cooking.

UNUSUAL AND INTERESTING ITEMS TAKEN FROM THE PARISH-REGISTERS

1614 - March 12th ye great snow broke wch had continewed from Friday seven weeks before.

Note - this year after the great snow followed a great drought which continewed the most part of somer.

1616 - May 4th Edward Astlie a poore man of Derby who died in in the parsonage barne ... was buried.

Ap. 3rd Elizabeth da. of Edward Allen bapt'd, ye said Edward Allen dwelling in Smalley Wood.

1618 - Memorand. that this yeare Novembr. the 25th and for three weeks after the blazing starre appeared in the East and did retrograde.

January 11th the White Hall was burned, and Queen Anne died the spring followinge.

1619 - Memo. that the 3 daie of Maie 1619 Rbt. Williamot of Chaddesden did cause a ditch to be digged upon Morley Lime wch. was presently cast in after them by appointment of Henry Sacheverel Esquire, Lord of Morley and so there was much to doe aboute nothing.

1635 - Nov. 18th Victorin Sacheverell gentleman brought forth of Wostershire and was buried at Morley.

1639 - Sept. 10th Anne Greine a wandering beggar woeman was buried in pt. by the women of Morley.

1656 - Jan. 22 Jacinth Sacheverell Lord of this Towne died in London, and was buried in Morley Church ye thirtieth day of the same month.

1682 - Mistres Elizab. S. above named relict. of Jonathas Esq. did give to this Church a communion cup and cover to it and did also give six pounds, the interest where of is to be imployed to the repaire of that part of the isle of the church to which hers and her husbands tombe stands and foure pounds more the interest where of is to be paid yearely to ye clarke for the keeping of there tombes in a decent manner from dust or any other defilements.

1684 - Oct. 20 Edward Martin buried wrapped in wollen.

1669 - Dec. 27 a child of Samuel Burrows whose name I know not and whether baptised or no I know not but by report.

1764 - In the years 64 and 63 the Revd. John Bakewell of Derby was Curate, and as he was a very negligent man and became afterwards insane, it is much to be feared that there were several omissions of entries in this register.

1781 - Nov. 14th Simon Wilmot Esq. buried aged 30 years. He was the 4th son of Rev. Rich'd Wilmot Rector of this Parish. In the Service of his King and Country in America he was wounded and then taken prisoner by the Rebels, and such was their cruelty to him that they suffered him to languish with his wounds undressed in a common prison for several days - this laid the foundation of the fatal disease a consumption of the lungs which brought him to his grave. He possessed a liberal mind, was generous brave and merciful.

1796 - June 18th Jane Holland buried aged 71, died it is supposed of a broken heart at her reduced state from competence to poverty. She was a worthy and good woman, but in her was an example of the folly of over indulgence of children to which may justly be atributed the miseries of the latter part of her life.

Nov. 8th Jane Mee buried aged 52 years. This woman had 13 children, all of them except one she suckled being very poor and of course ill supported in her nursing it ruined her constitution and brought on a Dropsy of which she died.

1794 - May 30th Jane Smith from Ramsay Huntingtonshire aged 58 yrs. buried - she died choked with fat.*

July 27th Mary Turner buried aged 16 yrs - she died after four days illness of a putrid fever (from drinking cold water and sitting in the cold when heated with washing).

Aug. 11th John Slater buried aged 24 yrs - his death was the same as Mary Turners, from taking cold after mowing?

1799 - August 13th Christopher Smith from Ramsay Huntingdonshire was buried aged 37 yrs - he died quite choked up with fat as did his mother in the year 94.*

1796 - Buried Rebecka Mason aged 90 yrs - the ouldest that I ever buried sins I was clark.
(added in a different hand) <u>you forget</u> John Day was as old.

1787 - Oct. 16th Thos Stanley buried aged 61 yrs. <u>Ale</u>

1803 - Oct. 2nd The Rev. Robert Wilmot, Rector of this Parish was buried aged 53 yrs. This funeral shewed an assembly of the whole Parish with tears and sadness on every face.

* Probably Goitre.

REFERENCES

1. "English Industries of the Middle Ages", L.F.Salzman 1964.
2. "History, Gazeteer and Directory of the County of Derby", S. Glover 1829, Volume 1, Part 1 Page 55.
3. "History, Gazeteer and Directory of the County of Derby", S. Glover 1829, Volume 1, Part 1 Page 186.
4. Reverend Robert Wilmot (1777 - 1803).
5. "The Place Names of Derbyshire", Dr.K.Cameron 1959, Volume 2 of 3.
6. P.H.Currey, Esq., F.R.I.B.A., Hon.Sec. Derbyshire Archaeological & Natural History Society 1901 - 1929.
7. Derbyshire Archaeological & Natural History Society, Volume 34 1912, pages 2 -3. (P.H.Currey).
8. Derbyshire Archaeological & Natural History Society, Volume 8, page 207 (W. Thompson Watkin).
9. "Victoria County History" Volume 1, 1905 Page 375 (W.Andrew).
10. J.W.Allen, Esq., F.G.S. Member Derbyshire Archaeological & Natural History Society.
11. R.W.P.Cockerton, Esq., LL.B., F.S.A. Member Derbyshire Archaeological & Natural History Society.
12. Reverend Samuel Fox (1844 - 1870) "History and Antiquities of the Church of St. Matthew Morley" 1872.
13. Mrs. Gwen Compton Bracebridge, wife of Reverend J. Compton Bracebridge (1938 - 1958) "A History of St. Matthew's Church Morley" 1949 (reprinted 1960).
14. "History & Gazeteer of Derbyshire" 1846.
15. F.S.Ogden, Esq., F.R.I.C.S. Churchwarden 1922 - 1977.
16. Reverend Charles Kerry, Rector of Smalley and author of "Smalley, History and Legends" Volume 1 1905, Volume 2 1907.
17. S. Bagshaw 1846.
18. "History, Gazeteer and Directory of the County of Derby" 1857, Francis White & Co.
19. "Old Church Gallery Minstrels" Canon K.H.McDermott 1948.
20. Reverend H.H. Bradshaw (1876 - ?)
21. Reverend C.J. Boden (1883 - 1917).
22. Reverend R.P. Stacy Waddy (1959 - 1966)
23. Reverend G.W. Burningham (1967 - 1972)

ACKNOWLEDGMENTS

In addition to those already mentioned in the preface, we wish to record our thanks to:-

Mrs. L. Giblin for the current maps of the village and drawings of The Almshouses, Three Horse Shoes, Morley Hall Gateway and the Butter Cross;

Mr. E.V.J. Bathurst, B.Sc., for the notes on Broomfield Hall;

the staff of Heanor County Library;

and all those who have kindly loaned photographs for inclusion in this History.

CONCLUSION

And so we come to the end of this short history of Morley, typical of many such English villages.

It has been said that a proper understanding of the past is the only sound basis on which to shape the future. Our studies have made us more aware of the community around us, shown us what a wealth of treasures we have inherited from the past, and made us realise that it is for us to preserve these and create in our own time a worthy addition, so that this portion of England's green and pleasant land will be as lovely for future generations as it is for us today.